Frommer's®

Amsterdam
day BY day®

3rd Edition

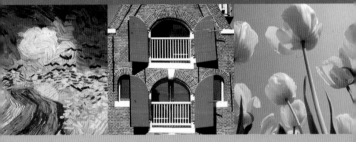

by George McDonald

WILEY

John Wiley & Sons, Inc.

Contents

Published by:

John Wiley & Sons, Inc.

111 River St.
Hoboken, NJ 07030-5774

ISBN 978-1-118-06630-0 (paper); ISBN 978-0-470-44475-7 (ebk);
ISBN 978-1-118-17222-3 (ebk); ISBN 978-1-118-17223-0 (ebk)

Editor: Jennifer Polland
Production Editor: Katie Robinson
Photo Editor: Cherie Cincilla
Cover Photo Editor: Richard Fox
Cartographer: Liz Puhl
Production by Wiley Indianapolis Composition Services

Front Cover: *Left:* Wheat Field with Crows (1890), Vincent van Gogh,
Van Gogh Museum, Amsterdam © SuperStock / SuperStock, Inc. *Middle:*
Canal houses, Amsterdam © Art Kowalsky / Alamy Images. *Right:* Tulips in
Keukenhof Gardens, Amsterdam © Keren Su / China Span / Alamy Images.
Back Cover: Leidseplein, cafe scene at night, Amsterdam © TTL Images /
Alamy Images.

For information on our other products and services or to obtain technical
support, please contact our Customer Care Department within the U.S.
at 877/762-2974, outside the U.S. at 317/572-3993 or fax 317/572-4002.

Wiley also publishes its books in a variety of electronic formats. Some
content that appears in print may not be available in electronic formats.

Manufactured in China

5 4 3 2 1

A Note from the Editorial Director

Organizing your time. That's what this guide is all about.

Other guides give you long lists of things to see and do and then expect you to fit the pieces together. The Day by Day guides are different. These guides tell you the best of everything, and then they show you how to see it in the *smartest, most time-efficient way*. Our authors have designed detailed itineraries organized by time, neighborhood, or special interest. And each tour comes with a bulleted map that takes you from stop to stop.

Hoping to admire some van Goghs, or buy some tulip bulbs to take back home? Planning to pedal along some canals, or take a whirl-wind tour of the very best that Amsterdam has to offer? Whatever your interest or schedule, the Day by Days give you the smartest routes to follow. Not only do we take you to the top attractions, hotels, and restaurants, but we also help you access those special moments that locals get to experience—those "finds" that turn tourists into travelers.

The Day by Days are also your top choice if you're looking for one complete guide for all your travel needs. The best hotels and res-taurants for every budget, the greatest shopping values, the wild-est nightlife—it's all here.

Why should you trust our judgment? Because our authors person-ally visit each place they write about. They're an independent lot who say what they think and would never include places they wouldn't recommend to their best friends. They're also open to suggestions from readers. If you'd like to contact them, please send your comments our way at frommersfeedback@wiley.com, and we'll pass them on.

Enjoy your Day by Day guide—the most helpful travel companion you can buy. And have the trip of a lifetime.

Warm regards,

Kelly Regan, Editorial Director
Frommer's Travel Guides

About the Author

George McDonald has lived and worked in Amsterdam as deputy editor of KLM's in-flight magazine, *Holland Herald*. Now a freelance journalist and travel writer, he has written extensively about Amsterdam and the Netherlands for magazines and travel books, including *Frommer's Amsterdam; Frommer's Belgium, Holland & Luxembourg; Frommer's Europe;* and *Europe For Dummies.*

Advisory & Disclaimer

Travel information can change quickly and unexpectedly, and we strongly advise you to confirm important details locally before traveling, including information on visas, health and safety, traffic and transport, accommodations, shopping, and eating out. We also encourage you to stay alert while traveling and to remain aware of your surroundings. Avoid civil disturbances, and keep a close eye on cameras, purses, wallets, and other valuables.

While we have endeavored to ensure that the information contained within this guide is accurate and up-to-date at the time of publication, we make no representations or warranties with respect to the accuracy or completeness of the contents of this work and specifically disclaim all warranties, including without limitation warranties of fitness for a particular purpose. We accept no responsibility or liability for any inaccuracy or errors or omissions, or for any inconvenience, loss, damage, costs, or expenses of any nature whatsoever incurred or suffered by anyone as a result of any advice or information contained in this guide.

The inclusion of a company, organization, or website in this guide as a service provider and/or potential source of further information does not mean that we endorse them or the information they provide. Be aware that information provided through some websites may be unreliable and can change without notice. Neither the publisher nor author shall be liable for any damages arising herefrom.

Star Ratings, Icons & Abbreviations

Every hotel, restaurant, and attraction listing in this guide has been ranked for quality, value, service, amenities, and special features using a **star-rating system.** Hotels, restaurants, attractions, shopping, and nightlife are rated on a scale of zero stars (recommended) to three stars (exceptional). In addition to the star-rating system, we also use a **kids icon** to point out the best bets for families. Within each tour, we recommend cafes, bars, or restaurants where you can take a break. Each of these stops appears in a shaded box marked with a coffee-cup-shaped bullet ☕ .

The following **abbreviations** are used for credit cards:

AE	American Express	DISC	Discover	V	Visa
DC	Diners Club	MC	MasterCard		

Frommers.com

Now that you have this guidebook to help you plan a great trip, visit our website at **www.frommers.com** for additional travel information on more than 4,000 destinations. We update features regularly to give you instant access to the most current trip-planning information available. At Frommers.com, you'll find scoops on the best airfares, lodging rates, and car rental bargains. You can even book your travel online through our reliable travel booking partners. Other popular features include:

- Online updates of our most popular guidebooks
- Vacation sweepstakes and contest giveaways
- Newsletters highlighting the hottest travel trends
- Podcasts, interactive maps, and up-to-the-minute events listings
- Opinionated blog entries by Arthur Frommer himself
- Online travel message boards with featured travel discussions

A Note on Prices

In the "Take a Break" and "Best Bets" sections of this book, we have used a system of dollar signs to show a range of costs for 1 night in a hotel (the price of a double-occupancy room) or the cost of an entree at a restaurant. Use the following table to decipher the dollar signs:

Cost	Hotels	Restaurants
$	under $100	under $10
$$	$100–$200	$10–$20
$$$	$200–$300	$20–$30
$$$$	$300–$400	$30–$40
$$$$$	over $400	over $40

An Invitation to the Reader

In researching this book, we discovered many wonderful places—hotels, restaurants, shops, and more. We're sure you'll find others. Please tell us about them, so we can share the information with your fellow travelers in upcoming editions. If you were disappointed with a recommendation, we'd love to know that, too. Please write to:

Frommer's Amsterdam Day by Day, 3rd Edition
John Wiley & Sons, Inc. • 111 River St. • Hoboken, NJ 07030-5774
frommersfeedback@wiley.com

13 Favorite
Moments

13 Favorite **Moments**

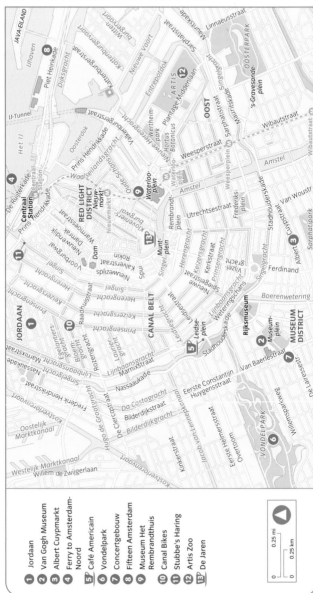

1 Jordaan
2 Van Gogh Museum
3 Albert Cuypmarkt
4 Ferry to Amsterdam-Noord
5 Café Americain
6 Vondelpark
7 Concertgebouw
8 Fifteen Amsterdam
9 Museum Het Rembrandthuis
10 Canal Bikes
11 Stubbe's Haring
12 Artis Zoo
13 De Jaren

Previous page: One of Amsterdam's idyllic canals at dusk.

So many of my favorite moments in Amsterdam are outdoors. Even in midwinter this city bustles with an infectious energy on its narrow streets, long canals, and many humpbacked bridges. Whichever time you choose to visit, you'll be struck, I'm sure, by how lively and bright this city really is. Here are some of my favorite moments, both outdoors and indoors, that have placed Amsterdam so close to my heart.

1 Strolling in the Jordaan. The first thing I do after arriving in Amsterdam—whether I'm here in the dead of winter or the brilliance of summer—is to take a long stroll in the Jordaan, up and down its beautiful tree-fringed canals. I like to look at the buildings and the houseboats, and then stop for a strong coffee at a neighborhood cafe. Then I'm ready for my first day in this vibrant and architecturally rich city. *See p 52.*

2 Admiring the paintings at the Van Gogh Museum, late in the afternoon just before the museum closes, is one of the highlights of a trip to Amsterdam. That's when the usually crowded second-floor gallery is almost empty and I can stand there, lost in my own world, admiring Vincent's brush strokes without being shoved around by the throngs. *See p 7.*

3 Picking out fruit at the Albert Cuyp Market, early in the morning (8–9am) as the many outdoor stands on this long street are being prepared for a day of shoppers, is a quintessential Amsterdam moment. I like to watch the fresh fish being laid out on ice, imagining how, not

You can see van Gogh's self-portrait and many other famous works at the Van Gogh Museum.

long ago, they were swimming in the North Sea. *See p 17.*

4 Catching the ferry to Amsterdam-Noord (North), from behind Centraal Station, immediately gives me a sense of space. The narrow Het IJ waterway is full of boats, ferries, and barges, and I ride the free ferry to the north bank and back, just to take in the views. *See p 40.*

Vondelpark is the perfect place to relax on a sunny day.

5 Living the Americain Dream, by taking coffee in the stunning Art Nouveau and Art Deco ambience of the Amsterdam American Hotel's Café Americain. Visitors will be pleased to learn that the service has improved considerably since a postwar Dutch writer dubbed the waiters here "unemployed knife throwers." *See p 85.*

Biking along Amsterdam's canals is a great way to get to know the city.

6 Strolling in Vondelpark on a sunny afternoon makes me feel as if I'm a million miles from any city. The English-style park is an echo of the countryside translated to the city, and when I'm lucky, I can stop and smell the roses, which bloom in late summer. *See p 78.*

7 An evening at the Concertgebouw, an acoustically perfect concert hall that many top conductors and orchestras visit, is one of my favorite ways to spend an evening in Amsterdam. *See p 116.*

8 Watching the hectic choreography of the waitstaff as they serve their trendy clientele at Jamie Oliver's restaurant Fifteen Amsterdam is mesmerizing. If you fail to make reservations, just sit at the bar and order appetizers (it's cheaper, anyway) as you take in the heady atmosphere of the young chefs in action in the open kitchen. *See p 96.*

9 Standing alone in Rembrandt's bedroom over 500 years after he last slept there fills me with awe. This is where he rested after a long day at the canvas, I think to myself over and over again. Come early in the day or right at closing time and you'll have a good chance at being alone, too. *See p 19.*

10 Peeking at houseboats at eye-level as I pedal a canal bike lets me see Amsterdam from a different angle. The Jordaan canals are especially dense with lived-in houseboats. *See p 83.*

11 Eating a raw herring with pickles and onions with the locals at Stubbe's Haring is what I do on my first day in Amsterdam. Somehow, the taste of the North Sea helps whet my appetite for all that's to come. *See p 15.*

12 A morning at the zoo makes me feel like a kid again. I walk to Artis Zoo, in the Plantage district east of the center city, to watch the animals being fed—a minisafari in the city. *See p 34.*

13 A frothy Grolsch beer at a waterside cafe at dusk is my favorite ending to any day in Amsterdam. I like to sit outside on the waterside terrace at De Jaren on Nieuwe Doelenstraat, and stretch my legs, watching the boats passing by on the Binnenamstel. *See p 106.* ●

Try some herring the way the locals eat it—with pickles and onions.

1

The Best **Full-Day Tours**

The Best in **One Day**

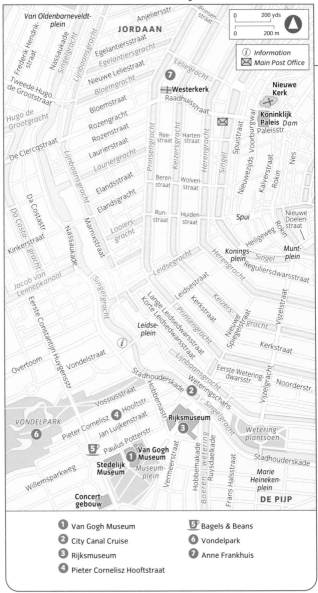

1 Van Gogh Museum
2 City Canal Cruise
3 Rijksmuseum
4 Pieter Cornelisz Hooftstraat
5 Bagels & Beans
6 Vondelpark
7 Anne Frankhuis

Previous page: Magere Brug (Skinny Bridge).

Amsterdam is a compact city, so this **1-day tour** allows you to see the major highlights with minimal time spent on public transportation. Wear comfortable shoes and be sure to look both ways as you cross major intersections—bicyclists follow no rules here and they travel at alarming speeds. START: **Tram 2, 3, 5, or 12 to Van Baerlestraat, or 16 or 24 to Museumplein.**

1 ★★★ Van Gogh Museum.

This gem of a museum houses the world's largest collection of Vincent van Gogh's work: 200 paintings, 580 drawings, and more than 700 letters by Vincent himself (most written to his brother, Theo). A four-story building (1973) designed by Gerrit Rietveld houses the permanent collection. Although most of the work here is by van Gogh, the third floor includes paintings by Impressionist artists such as Monet, Seurat, Pissarro, Gauguin, and Toulouse-Lautrec. An adjacent annex (1999) in the shape of an ellipse, designed by Japanese "organic" architect Kisho Kurokawa, houses temporary exhibits. These change every 3 or 4 months, and often include some of van Gogh's drawings. ⏱ *3 hr. Paulus Potterstraat 7 (at Museumplein).* ☎ *020/570-5200. www.vangogh museum.nl. Admission 14€ adults, free for kids under 18. Sat–Thurs 10am–6pm; Fri 10am–10pm. Closed Jan 1. Tram: 2, 3, 5, or 12 to Van Baerlestraat; 16 or 24 to Museumplein.*

Touring Amsterdam by canal boat can help you get a feel for the city.

2 ★★ City Canal Cruise.

There's no better way to discover Amsterdam than from its canals. Sure, it's touristy, but I can't think of a better way to see much of Amsterdam in a short time. You can opt to sit outside (on some boats) or settle into a

Vermeer's The Kitchen Maid, *at the Rijksmuseum.*

comfortable seat indoors. A typical cruise, for instance with the Blue Boat Company, will loop northward on the western canals, circle Centraal Station, and loop back to the departure point along the eastern canals. There's commentary in English, so you'll know what you're seeing. ⏱ *1¼ hr. Stadhouderskade 30 (at Leidseplein).* ☎ *020/679-1370. www.blueboat.nl. Tickets 13€ adults, 7€ kids 5–12 (prices may vary from line to line). Departures every 30 min. 10am–6pm and at 7pm Apr–Sept; every hr. 10am–5pm Oct–Mar. Tram: 1, 2, 5, 7, or 10 to Leidseplein.*

Avid shoppers will want to head to Pieter Cornelisz Hooftstraat for upscale shops and boutiques.

3 ★★★ Rijksmuseum. Architect Petrus Josephus Hubertus Cuypers designed this museum in a monumental Dutch neo-Renaissance style. Cuypers, a Catholic, slipped in more than a dab of neo-Gothic, too, causing the country's Protestant king William III to scorn what he called "that cathedral." The building opened in 1885. Most of the museum is closed for major renovations until 2013, but a section of the museum, the Philips Wing, remains open throughout the renovation to showcase "the Masterpieces"—the museum's highlights, primarily from the period of Holland's 17th-century "Golden Age." Rembrandt and Vermeer lovers, don't panic: You can still see *The Night Watch* and *The Kitchen Maid*. In fact, you'll find an entire room filled with Rembrandts. Three other galleries are dedicated to Vermeer, Frans Hals, and Jan Steen. ⏲ 1½ hr. *Jan Luijkenstraat 1 (at Museumplein).* ☎ *020/674-7000. www.rijksmuseum.nl. Admission 13€ adults, free for kids under 19. Sat–Thurs 9am–6pm; Fri 9am–8:30pm. Closed Jan 1. Tram: 2 or 5 to Hobbemastraat.*

4 ★ Pieter Cornelisz Hoofts-traat. The city's most upscale shopping district lies just a block from the Rijksmuseum, so those with shopping aspirations should take advantage of the opportunity to spend an hour strolling the short but oh-so-chic P.C.

Hooftstraat (locals usually shorten the name to "P.C. Hooft"). You'll find the quintessential jet-set boutiques such as Louis Vuitton, Armani, Ralph Lauren, and Gucci clustered on this primo stretch of real estate; you can even pick up a diamond from Tiffany & Co. ⏲ 30–60 min. *Shops open Mon–Sat 10am–6pm. Tram: 2 or 5 to Hobbemastraat.*

5 Bagels & Beans. This sit-down snack bar belonging to the trendy Dutch franchise chain serves an array of bagels and coffee drinks. To these you can add omelets, muffins, iced teas, freshly pressed fruit juices, and more—some of them organic. *Van Baerlestraat 40 (at Willemsparkweg).* ☎ *020/675-7050. $.*

6 ★★ Vondelpark. A 2-minute stroll from the Rijksmuseum and P.C. Hooftstraat brings you to the largest and most popular park in Amsterdam. Vondelpark is 44 hectares (109 acres) of peace and quiet, a cherished open space speckled with trees in this terribly dense city. Benches overlook small ponds, walking trails, and bike trails. See also the tour of Vondelpark on p 78. ⏲ 30 min. *Enter through the gate on Van Eeghenlaan, at the corner of Jacob Obrechtstraat. Open 24 hr. Tram: 2, 3, 5, or 12 to Van Baerlestraat.*

Van Gogh: 10 Years of Genius

The second floor of the Van Gogh Museum's permanent exhibit gives you a fascinating chronological insight into van Gogh's life and work. Although his career as a painter lasted only 10 years—during which time he completed over 900 paintings—you'll see stunning shifts in style and color as you move from one year and one geographical area to another. For example, compare the dark and somber *Potato Eaters* from his earliest work in Holland in 1885 to the light and airy *View of the Roofs of Paris,* completed just a year later.

The paintings van Gogh completed in Arles—like his famous *Bedroom at Arles* (1888)—explode with color. There are several lesser-known paintings from the last year of his life, including the ominous *Wheatfield Under Thundercloud,* painted shortly before his suicide in 1890.

⑦ ★★★ Anne Frankhuis. It's about a 30-minute walk from Vondelpark to the Anne Frank House (or you can catch a tram). It was in this typical Amsterdam canal house that a 13-year-old Anne Frank began to keep her famous diary. For 2 years during World War II, the Frank family and other Jewish refugees hid in near-total silence in these rooms, before they were betrayed and Nazi forces raided the house and deported them to concentration camps. You can see where young Anne pinned up photos of her favorite actress, Deanna Durbin, and view an original copy of Anne's diary. Protective Plexiglas panels have been placed over some walls, but little else has changed since the Franks lived here—though a 2010 storm brought down the old chestnut tree in a neighboring garden that Anne loved so much. Almost a million visitors a year tour this house; be prepared to spend some time waiting to enter. If you have enough time, take in a related exhibit in the extended museum. ⏱ 1½ hr. Arrive after 4pm to avoid long lines, especially in summer. Prinsengracht 263–267 (at Westermarkt). ☎ 020/556-7105.

www.annefrank.org. Admission 8.50€ adults, 4€ kids 10–17. Mid-Mar to June and 1st 2 weeks in Sept Sun–Fri 9am–9pm, Sat 9am–10pm; July–Aug daily 9am–10pm; mid-Sept to mid-Mar Sun–Fri 9am–7pm, Sat 9am–9pm. Closed Yom Kippur. Tram: 13, 14, or 17 to Westermarkt.

The bookcase door that led to Anne Frank's hiding place.

The Best in **Two Days**

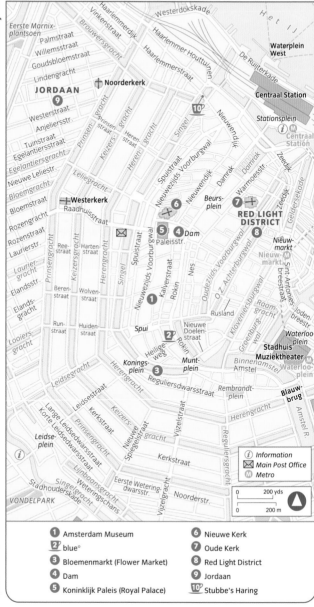

1 Amsterdam Museum
2' blue°
3 Bloemenmarkt (Flower Market)
4 Dam
5 Koninklijk Paleis (Royal Palace)
6 Nieuwe Kerk
7 Oude Kerk
8 Red Light District
9 Jordaan
10' Stubbe's Haring

If you followed the **"Best in One Day"** tour, then you've already visited the most popular attractions and gotten an overview of the city from a canal cruise. Today you'll dig further into Amsterdam's history and architecture by visiting some of its monuments, smaller museums, and neighborhoods. You'll also stroll around the Flower Market and take a peek at the infamous Red Light District. START: **Tram: 1, 2, 4, 5, 9, 14, 16, 24, or 25 to Spui.**

1 ★★ Amsterdam Museum.

This museum will give you fascinating insights into the city of Amsterdam. The museum is housed in a former orphanage dating to the 17th century (a small part of it dates to 1578, when it was a convent). Gallery by gallery, century by century, you learn how a small fishing village founded around 1200 became a major sea power and trading center. Many exhibits focus on the city's glittering 17th-century *Gouden Eeuw* (Golden Age). Art lovers will enjoy seeing famous paintings by Dutch masters explained in the context of their time and place in history. An intricate scale model from 1677 shows what is now the Royal Palace (stop 5 on this tour). In summer, you can dine outdoors under the shade of courtyard trees at the museum's **Museumcafé Mokum.** See also the **Schuttersgalerij (Civic Guards Gallery;** p 24). 🕐 *2 hr. Kalverstraat 92, Nieuwezijds Voorburgwal 357, and Sint-Luciënsteeg 27.*

☎ *020/523-1822. www.amsterdam museum.nl. Admission 10€ adults, 5€ kids 6–18. Mon–Fri 10am–5pm; Sat–Sun and holidays 11am–5pm. Closed Jan 1, Apr 30, Dec 25. Tram: 1, 2, 4, 5, 9, 14, 16, 24, or 25 to Spui.*

2 ★ blue°.

I love to stop at the Kalvertoren mall for a late breakfast and take in the heavenly 360-degree views of Amsterdam. If the weather is fine, you can grab a seat on the top-floor terrace, but the views from the floor-to-ceiling windows in the expansive lower dining room are equally panoramic. *The Kalvertoren; enter on Singel 457 and take the elevator to the 3rd floor.* ☎ *020/427-3901. $$.*

3 ★ Bloemenmarkt (Flower Market).

Since you're in the heart of Amsterdam's main shopping street, Kalverstraat, you may want to spend some time browsing. When

An exhibit from the Amsterdam Museum.

The Dam.

you've had your fill, head two streets south to the Singel canal (at Muntplein). You'll find the Flower Market, which partially floats on a row of permanently moored barges, exploding with color and hundreds of flowers. *Singel (at Muntplein). Mon–Sat 9am–5:30pm; Sun 11am–5:30pm. Tram: 4, 9, 14, 16, 24, or 25 to Muntplein.*

You'll find a large variety of flowers, including lots of tulips, at the Bloemenmarkt.

④ ★★ **Dam.** The Dam is the square that's the epicenter of Amsterdam. It's the site of the original dam built across the Amstel River in the 13th century, hence the name. It isn't particularly grand (and it's always busy), but several of the city's important monuments can be found here: the **Koninklijk Paleis, Nationaal Monument,** and the **Nieuwe Kerk.** Take a walk around the Nationaal Monument, a white column erected in 1956 as a tribute to Dutch citizens who died during the Nazi occupation during World War II. Urns filled with soil from the then 11 provinces of the Netherlands and its former colonial possession, the Dutch East Indies (Indonesia), sit behind the monument. ⏱ *15 min. Tram: 1, 2, 4, 5, 9, 13, 14, 16, 17, 24, or 25 to the Dam.*

⑤ ★ **Koninklijk Paleis (Royal Palace).** This is still the official residence of the reigning king or queen of the Netherlands, though Queen Beatrix and the other scions of the House of Orange prefer to live in The Hague. The palace (1648–55), originally designed as Amsterdam's Town Hall, has a solid, neoclassical facade. The building didn't become a palace until 1808. Its interior is filled with early-19th-century furniture, chandeliers, and marble floors. Among the most magnificent rooms are the high-ceilinged Burgerzaal (Citizens' Chamber), where the maps inlaid on the marble floors show Amsterdam as the center of the world, and the ornate Vierschaar (Court of Justice). The palace is closed to visitors during periods of royal residence and state receptions. 🕐 *1 hr. Dam.* ☎ *020/620-4060. www.paleisamsterdam.nl. Admission 7.50€ adults; 6.50€ seniors, students & kids 5–16. July–Aug daily 11am–5pm; Sept–June irregularly noon–5pm (days & hours are posted on the website, but may vary with little or no notice; check before going).*

Koninklijk Paleis (Royal Palace).

⑥ ★ Nieuwe Kerk (New Church). Originally built in the 15th century—construction started in 1410—as the city's second Catholic Church, the Nieuwe Kerk was largely destroyed by fire in the 17th century. (Look for the carved gilded ceiling above the choir, which survived.) A great deal of its original neo-Gothic grandeur has been restored, and all

One of the Nieuwe Kerk's (New Church's) elaborate stained-glass windows.

Dutch monarchs are inaugurated (not crowned!) here. Don't miss the elaborately carved altar and the great pipe organ (from about 1645), which is still used for concerts. In the south transept, the lower-right corner of the stained-glass windows depicts Queen Wilhelmina surrounded by courtiers at her inauguration. 🕐 *30 min. Dam (next to the Royal Palace).* ☎ *020/638-6909. www.nieuwekerk.nl. Admission varies with different events; free when there's no special exhibit. Daily 10am–6pm.*

⑦ ★★ Oude Kerk (Old Church). A walk of several blocks east from the Nieuwe Kerk (into the Red Light District) brings you to the late-Gothic, triple-nave church, which was begun in 1250 and completed with the extension of the bell tower in 1566. Rembrandt's wife lies in vault 28K, which bears the simple inscription "Saskia Juni 1642." The magnificent 1728 open organ is regularly used for recitals. You can climb the church tower on a half-hourly guided tour (in English) for a great view of Old Amsterdam and the adjacent Red Light District. 🕐 *30 min. Oudekerksplein (at Oudezijds Voorburgwal).*

The Royal Household

Although Queen Beatrix's official residence is the Royal Palace, she does not own it, nor does she own any of her other residences. The state makes them available to her and allocates a budget of about 40 million euros per year to manage her royal household. Her salary is separate. She pays taxes only on her private assets—which, though difficult to calculate, are not substantial enough to make her one of the richest women in the world, as was once thought.

☎ 020/625-8284 church; 020/689-2565 tower. www.oudekerk.nl. Church: Admission 5€ adults; 4€ seniors, students & kids 13–18. Mon–Sat 11am–5pm; Sun 1–5pm. Tower: Admission 6€; minimum age 12. Apr–Sept Thurs–Sat 1–5pm. Closed Jan 1, Apr 30 & Dec 25. Metro: Nieuwmarkt.

⑧ Red Light District. Amsterdam's *Rosse Buurt* (Red Light District) is one of its best-known "attractions," with red lights illuminating minimally clad prostitutes on display behind glass windows along medieval canals

The Oude Kerk (Old Church).

and alleyways. There are also live, hard-core sex shows that leave nothing to the imagination. Some visitors are repulsed by the sight of flesh for sale; for others it's just a fascinating window into the world's oldest profession. The Oude Kerk is in the middle of the Red Light District, so you can simply cross the canal and stroll up and down Oudezijds Achterburgwal. Just outside the Oude Kerk is what's claimed to be the world's first monument to prostitution. The bronze sculpture *Belle* (2007) depicts a hooker standing in a doorway and bears an inscription calling for "respect for sexworkers [sic] all over the world." It's safe to meander here. You can skip it and head northwest from the Oude Kerk to Warmoesstraat, a pedestrian-only street lined with bars, funky sex shops (among them a "condomerie"), and "coffee shops" where patrons are more likely to order marijuana than coffee. From Oudezijds Achterburgwal, head back toward the Oude Kerk, cross Oudezijds Voorburgwal and you'll hit Warmoesstraat. Continue along the street and you'll find yourself facing Centraal Station.
⏱ 15–30 min. Dusk is the best time to visit, though it's open 24 hr. Metro: Nieuwmarkt.

⑨ ★★ Jordaan. It feels miles away from the crowded, sometimes seedy center city where you've

The Red Light District at night.

spent most of the day, yet the Jordaan is almost adjacent to Centraal Station and a great place to relax after a day of sightseeing. It's the most hip and unpretentiously elegant neighborhood in all of Amsterdam, its discreet canals lined with houseboats and its streets full of quaint boutiques and delightful cafes. If you have the time and energy, check out the walking tour of the Jordaan (p 52).

🔟 **Stubbe's Haring.** Raw herring is a Dutch specialty, and there are dozens of haringhuis fish stands in town. This stand, located on a bridge on the way from the Jordaan to Centraal Station, is (arguably) the top place in town. It's a great spot for "new herring" and other seafood snacks. *Nieuwe Haarlemmersluis (at Singel).* ☎ *020/623-3212. $.*

A Behind-the-Scenes Look at the Dutch Sex Industry

The Red Light District in Amsterdam dates back to the 13th century, when the city emerged as Europe's leading port and sailors returned from long trips desperate for female companionship. By 1850, with a little over 200,000 residents in the city, there were already more than 200 brothels. To this day, there's debate within the government as to how to regulate this industry. In recent years, the city has been acting to rein in the sex industry and its links to organized crime, drugs, and human trafficking, by cutting the number of prostitutes' windows and sex clubs, and encouraging the spread of "normal" life in the Red Light District. Recent statistics claim that more than 60% of the women working in the sex industry are foreign, the majority of them new migrants from Eastern Europe and Asia. They can expect to earn 60€ to 150€ per customer, depending on what is asked of them. High-class prostitutes (found through an upmarket escort service or luxury brothel) can pull in over 1,000€ a night.

The Best in **Three Days**

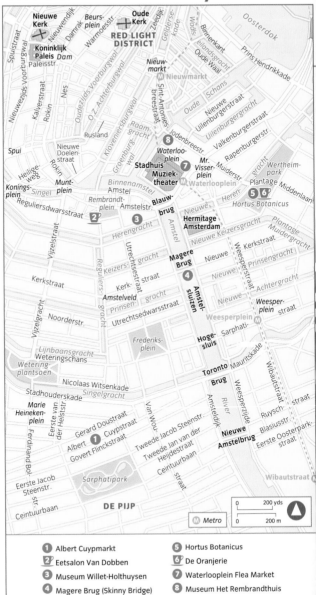

1. Albert Cuypmarkt
2. Eetsalon Van Dobben
3. Museum Willet-Holthuysen
4. Magere Brug (Skinny Bridge)
5. Hortus Botanicus
6. De Oranjerie
7. Waterlooplein Flea Market
8. Museum Het Rembrandthuis

If you've followed the "Best in One" and "Best in Two Days" tours, then you've already seen many of the city's highlights. It's time to slow down a bit, blend in with the locals, meander around the markets, and take in some smaller museums. On this tour, you'll also get a chance to (literally) stop and smell the roses at the relaxing Botanical Garden. START: **Tram 4, 16, 24, or 25 to Albert Cuypstraat.**

You can find fresh cheese, fish, fruit, vegetables, and more at the Albert Cuypmarkt.

① ★ **Albert Cuypmarkt.** I love coming to the Albert Cuyp Market in the morning, getting lost in the frenzy of shoppers, and marveling at the rows of fresh fish, fruit, vegetables, and textiles on display. The street market lies along Albert Cuypstraat in the heart of De Pijp, a residential neighborhood that has a mixed population of young professionals and ethnic minorities, many of the latter hailing (though it may be several generations back) from the former Dutch colony of Suriname. The area is slightly more affordable than the Jordaan and therefore attracts a somewhat younger crowd. Along the streets that intersect Albert Cuypstraat, you'll find many cafes where you can get a quick pick-me-up of strong coffee or tea. ⏱ *1 hr. Albert Cuypstraat, btw. Van Woustraat & Ferdinand Bolstraat. Mon–Sat 9am–6pm. Tram 4, 16, 24, or 25 to Albert Cuypstraat.*

Fun Facts & Figures

In Amsterdam, you'll find 760,000 permanent residents; more than a million visitors each month; 600,000 flower bulbs in its parks and public gardens; 1,281 bridges (8 of them wooden drawbridges); 600,000 bicycles; 220,000 trees; 260 city trams; 6,800 16th-, 17th-, and 18th-century buildings; 2,400 houseboats; 1,400 cafes and bars; 755 restaurants; 206 paintings by van Gogh; and 22 paintings by Rembrandt.

A period room from the Museum Willet-Holthuysen.

2 **Eetsalon Van Dobben.** Though this is more of a sandwich place, some patrons swear by the platter of giant meatballs. Locals come here for herring, liverwurst, croquets, or ox-tongue sandwiches, served from a marble counter. *Korte Reguliersdwarsstraat 5–9 (off Rembrandtplein).* ☎ *020/624-4200. $.*

3 ★ **Museum Willet-Holthuysen.** This is one of the best-preserved 17th-century canal houses in Amsterdam. It was built in 1687 and renovated several times before its last owner, Louisa Willet-Holthuysen, willed the mansion and her fine-art collection to the city in 1885.

Among the most interesting rooms are a Victorian-era bedroom on the second floor, a large reception room with tapestry wall panels, and an 18th-century basement kitchen set up to look as though the cook has just stepped out to go shopping. Be sure to peek out at the impressively restored 18th-century formal garden. ⏱ *45 min. Herengracht 605 (near the Amstel River).* ☎ *020/523-1822. www.willetholthuysen.nl. Admission 8€ adults, 4€ kids 6–18. Mon–Fri 10am–5pm; Sat–Sun & holidays 11am–5pm. Closed Jan 1, Apr 30 & Dec 25. Tram: 4, 9, or 14 to Rembrandtplein.*

4 ★ **Magere Brug (Skinny Bridge).** After leaving the museum, head west toward the Amstel, then south along the riverbank for a quick 15-minute detour to see this fantastic bridge. Legend has it that the Magere Brug was built to make it easier for two sisters (of the Mager family) who lived on opposite sides of the river to visit each other—but *mager* also means "thin" in Dutch, hence the nickname. The double drawbridge was built in 1670 of African azobé wood; it was last renovated in 1969. Come during the day to see the unusual wood details, or at night to see it twinkling with hundreds of lights. ⏱ *15 min. The bridge spans the Amstel btw. Kerkstraat & Nieuwe Kerkstraat.*

The Magere Brug (Skinny Bridge) at night.

5 ★ **kids** **Hortus Botanicus (Botanical Garden).** On the right (east) bank of the river, go northeast to this oasis of green, a treasure-trove of tropical plants taken from (among other places) the former Dutch colonies of Indonesia, Suriname, and the Antilles. Established in 1682, this lovely garden explodes with the colors and scents of more than 250,000 flowers and 115,000 plants and trees. The city's physicians and apothecaries originally created it as a garden for medicinal herbs. The first coffee plant in Europe was brought here in 1706 by a Dutch merchant who smuggled it out of Ethiopia. The tri-climate greenhouse gets progressively warmer as you walk through it—most of the plants here come from Australia and South Africa. There's also an herb garden, a desert greenhouse, and a butterfly house with free-flying giant butterflies that kids will love. ⌚ *1 hr. Plantage Middenlaan 2A.* ☎ *020/625-9021. www. dehortus.nl. Admission 7.50€ adults, 3.50€ seniors & kids 5–14. Feb–June & Sept–Nov Mon–Fri 9am–5pm, Sat–Sun 10am–5pm; July–Aug Mon–Fri 9am–7pm, Sat–Sun & holidays 10am–7pm; Dec–Jan Mon–Fri 9am–4pm, Sat–Sun & holidays 10am–4pm. Closed Jan 1, Sept 30 & Dec 25. Tram: 9 or 14 to Plantage Kerklaan.*

6 ★ **De Oranjerie.** This cafe, in Hortus Botanicus, is one of my favorite places to unwind and recharge. It's housed in the beautiful 1875 Oranjerie building, designed to shelter citrus trees in winter. The cafe serves one of the best apple pies in the city, along with delicious salads and imaginative sandwiches. If you score one of the outdoor tables, you can listen to the birds chirping as you eat. *Inside Hortus Botanicus, Plantage Middenlaan 2A.* ☎ *020/625-9021. $$.*

7 ★ **Waterlooplein Flea Market.** Another 10-minute walk brings you to this quintessentially classic Amsterdam flea market. In its glory, before World War II, amazing antiques could be found and maybe even paintings by the masters at bargain prices. Today you can meander from one merchant's tent to another, hunting for good deals on anything from cooking pots to used CDs, leather jackets, watches, and colorful sweaters. I come here just to people-watch. It's also a good place to try some street food, like french fries eaten Dutch style—with mayonnaise. ⌚ *30 min. Waterlooplein. Mon–Sat 10am–5pm. Tram: 9 or 14 to Waterlooplein.*

8 ★★ **Museum Het Rembrandthuis (Rembrandt House Museum).** Just around the corner from Waterlooplein lies the beautifully preserved house from 1606 where the artist Rembrandt van Rijn lived and worked in the 17th century. He bought the three-story house in 1639 when he was Amsterdam's most fashionable portrait painter. In this house, Rembrandt's son Titus was born and his wife Saskia died. Due to his extravagant lifestyle, Rembrandt was bankrupt when he left the house in 1658, and it wasn't until

You'll find lots of Dutch wares, like these mini porcelain clogs, at the Waterlooplein Flea Market.

Amsterdam for **Art Lovers**

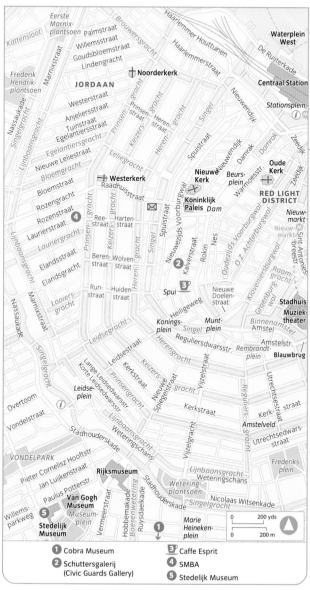

Eerste Marnix-plantsoen
Kattensloot
Palmstraat
Brouwersgracht
Haarlemmer Houttuinen
Haarlemmerstraat
Waterplein West
De Ruijterkade
Willemsstraat
Marnixstraat
Goudsbloemstraat
Lindengracht
Frederik Hendrik-plantsoen
Noorderkerk
Centraal Station
JORDAAN
Stationsplein
Nassaukade
Singelgracht
Lijnbaansgracht
Marnixstraat
Westerstraat
Anjeliersstraat
Tuinstraat
Egelantiersstraat
Prinsen- straat
Heren- straat
Keizers- gracht
Prinsen- gracht
Heren- gracht
Singel
Nieuwe Leliestraat
Egelantiersgracht
Leliegracht
Nieuwendijk
Nieuwezijds Voorburgwal
Spuistraat
Bloemgracht
Westerkerk
Nieuwe Kerk
Oude Kerk
Beurs-plein
Zeedijk
Bloemstraat
Raadhuisstraat
Damrak
Warmoesstraat
RED LIGHT DISTRICT
Rozengracht
Koninklijk Paleis Dam
Nieuw-markt
Rozenstraat
Ree-straat
Harten-straat
Nieuwezijds Voorburgwal
O.Z. Achterburgwal
Oudezijds Voorburgwal
Sint-Antonies-breestr.
Laurierstraat
Lauriergracht
Prinsengracht
Keizersgracht
Herengracht
Singel
Kalverstraat
Rokin
Nes
Kloveniersburgwal
Raam-gracht
Groenburg
Elandsstraat
Beren-straat
Wolven-straat
Stadhuis
Muziek-theater
Elandsgracht
Run-straat
Huiden-straat
Spui
Nieuwe Doelen-straat
Binnen Amstel
Lijnbaansgracht
Marnixstraat
Looiers-gracht
Heren-gracht
Helligeweg
Konings-plein
Munt-plein
Amstelstr.
Blauwbrug
Nassaukade
Singelgracht
Leidsegracht
Singel
Herengracht
Reguliersdwarsstr.
Rembrandt-plein
Overtoom
Lange Leidsedwarsstr.
Korte Leidsedwarsstr.
Leidsestraat
Kerkstraat
Prinsengracht
Keizers-gracht
Nieuwe Spiegelstraat
Reguliers-gracht
Vijzelgracht
Vijzelstraat
Utrechtsestraat
Kerk-straat
Utrechtsedwars-straat
Vondelstraat
Leidse-plein
Kerkstraat
Amstelveld
VONDELPARK
Stadhouderskade
Lijnbaansgracht
Weteringschans
Frederiks-plein
Pieter Cornelisz Hooftstr.
Jan Luijkenstraat
Paulus Potterstr.
Rijksmuseum
Wetering-plantsoen
Weteringschans
Nicolaas Witsenkade
Singelgracht
Willems-parkweg
Van Gogh Museum
Hobbemakade
Boerenwetering
Stadhouderskade
Ruysdaelkade
Vermeerstraat
Museum-plein
Stedelijk Museum
Marie Heineken-plein
0   200 yds
0   200 m

① Cobra Museum
② Schuttersgalerij (Civic Guards Gallery)
③ Caffe Esprit
④ SMBA
⑤ Stedelijk Museum

Previous page: The modern façade of Science Center NEMO.

Amsterdam is a feast for art lovers. With more than 20 Rembrandts, more than 200 van Goghs, numerous Vermeers, and a plethora of Impressionist and post-Impressionist paintings scattered throughout the city, art lovers will be in heaven here. This tour is for art lovers who would have already made a beeline to the top museums and are ready to dig deeper into all the art riches that Amsterdam has to offer. Today you'll have a chance to see contemporary works by local, living artists; the Stedelijk Museum's incredible collection of modern art; and the Schuttersgalerij, with its outsized canvases depicting well-to-do members of 17th-century Civic Guards companies. START: **Cobra Museum (Amstelveen); tram 5 to Amstelveen Binnenhof or Metro line 51 to Amstelveen Centrum.**

An exhibit from the Cobra Museum.

1 ★ Cobra Museum. Art lovers will find this breathtakingly modern museum worth the trek to its off-the-beaten-path location. (I recommend taking a 15-min. taxi ride or 20-min. tram ride from the center city straight here and back—leafy, suburban Amstelveen is not the most scenic area of Amsterdam.) The museum (1995), designed by Dutch architect Wim Quist, overflows with the post–World War II abstract expressionist art of the Cobra group, named for the initials of the founding artists' home cities: *Co*penhagen, *Br*ussels, and Amsterdam. Karel Appel (1921–2006) was the Dutchman, a controversial painter, sculptor, and graphic artist. As is true of many Cobra artists, Appel's work, including *Child and Beast II* (1951), has a childlike quality, employing bright colors and abstract shapes. He once said, "I paint like a barbarian in a barbarous age." The building's abundant natural light and open space creates a perfect home for the modern art

An exhibit from the SMBA.

found here. ⏱ *2 hr. Sandbergplein 1, Amstelveen.* ☎ *020/547-5050. www. cobra-museum.nl. Admission 9.50€ adults, 6.50€ seniors, 5€ students & kids 6–18. Tues–Sun & holidays (including holiday Mon) 11am–5pm. Closed Jan 1, Apr 30 & Dec 25. Tram: 5 to Amstelveen Binnenhof. Metro: Line 51 to Amstelveen Centrum.*

❷ Schuttersgalerij (Civic Guards Gallery). Stroll through this narrow, sky-lit passageway just outside the **Amsterdam Museum** (p 11), linking Kalverstraat to the **Begijnhof** (p 61). Under the walkway's glass roof, you'll see 15 bigger-is-better, 17th-century paintings showing the city's heroic musketeers, the Civic Guards. Elegantly uniformed and coiffed, these militia companies once played an important role in the city's defense, but degenerated into little more than banqueting societies. The paintings are in the same tradition, if not quite the same league, as Rembrandt's *The Night Watch,* but then you don't have to line up and pay to view them. And seen in this relaxed context, without crowds, they are well worth the detour. One of the best is *Captain Joan Huydecoper's Company Celebrating the Peace of Münster* (1648), by Govert Flinck. ⏱ *20*

min. At Amsterdam Museum, btw. Sint-Luciënsteeg and Gedempte Begijnensloot. ☎ *020/523-1822. www. amsterdammuseum.nl. Free admission. Mon–Fri 10am–5pm; Sat–Sun & holidays 11am–5pm; Closed Jan 1. Tram: 1, 2, 4, 5, 9, 16, 24, or 25 to Spui.*

❸ Caffe Esprit. Diners come here for the cool interior and one of Amsterdam's most desirable outdoor terraces—not the food. Stick to typical cafe fare—coffee, sandwiches, and salads—and you should do okay. *Spui 10 (outside the Begijnhof).* ☎ *020/622-1967. $.*

❹ SMBA. Head to the Jordaan district (take tram 14 from the Spui stop on Rokin), to take in this initiative by the city's modern-art Stedelijk Museum (see below). The innovative gallery was described in a Dutch newspaper as a "hatchery for young artistic talent," and it primarily showcases young artists from Amsterdam. Exhibits change regularly, and the works are by promising young artists who embrace painting, sculpture, video, installations, or performance art. ⏱ *45 min. Rozenstraat 59 (off Prinsengracht).* ☎ *020/422-0471.*

An exhibit from the Stedelijk Museum.

www.smba.nl. Free admission. Tues–Sun 11am–5pm. Closed Jan 1, Apr 30 & Dec 25. Tram: 13, 14, or 17 to Westermarkt.

5 ★★ **Stedelijk Museum.** Amsterdam's premier modern-art gallery (either do the long walk there, or get to the Dam or Leidseplein and ride tram 2 or 5), with its collection devoted primarily to post–World War II art, won't fully re-open until the end of 2011 after a long period of rebuilding and refurbishment. You'll then likely see works by Karel Appel, Andy Warhol, Willem de Kooning, and Piet Mondrian, among others. The Stedelijk owns the largest collection outside of Russia of the abstract paintings of Kazimir Malevich. Not all of the collection is on display all the time, and it's possible that you won't see many—or even any—of these. You can count on seeing examples from the Cobra, post-Cobra, *nouveau realisme,* pop art, color-field painting, zero, minimalist, and conceptual schools of modern art. In addition, there are three van Goghs: *Montmartre* (1887), *Carnations* (1888), and *The Diggers* (1889); and a small collection of paintings by Chagall, Cézanne, Picasso, and Renoir. Despite the names mentioned here, the Stedelijk is not the place to see van Goghs or works by French Impressionists. ⏱ *2 hr. Paulus Potterstraat 13 (at Museumplein).* ☎ *020/573-2911. www.stedelijk.nl. The following prices and hours may change when the museum reopens fully. Admission 10€ adults, 5€ students & kids 13–18, 20€ family. Tues–Wed & Fri–Sun 10am–5pm; Thurs 10am–10pm. Closed Jan 1. Tram: 2, 3, 5, or 12 to Van Baerlestraat; 16 or 24 to Museumplein.*

City of van Gogh

Vincent has never had it so good. His paintings sell for stratospheric amounts and exhibits of his work draw huge crowds. Amsterdam is the world center of the Vincent cult, and the Van Gogh Museum (p 7) is its temple. Nowhere else are so many paintings by the 19th-century artist displayed, and in chronological order, allowing visitors to track his progress. These are accompanied by drawings, sketches, and voluminous correspondence with his brother Theo.

Architectural Amsterdam

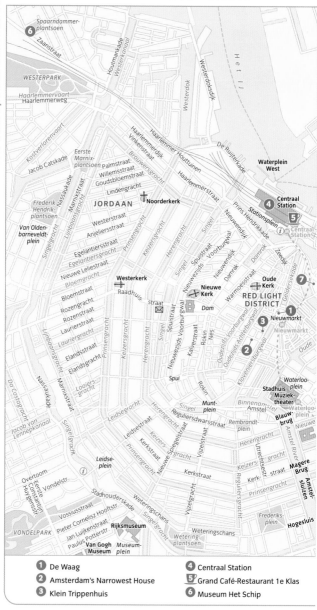

1 De Waag

2 Amsterdam's Narrowest House

3 Klein Trippenhuis

4 Centraal Station

5 Grand Café-Restaurant 1e Klas

6 Museum Het Schip

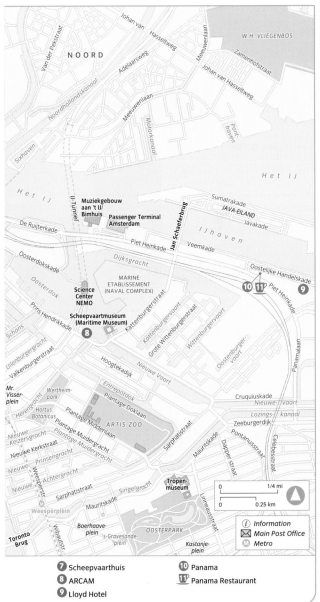

7 Scheepvaarthuis
8 ARCAM
9 Lloyd Hotel
10 Panama
11 Panama Restaurant

i Information
✉ Main Post Office
Ⓜ Metro

There are so many architectural styles in Amsterdam that the city can seem quite schizophrenic at times. Architecture buffs can entertain themselves just by walking the streets or taking a tram ride in any corner of the city. On this tour, you'll get an overview of the major schools of architecture, starting with medieval, but I've focused on examples from the Amsterdam School, the unique movement that forever changed the look of the city in the early decades of the 20th century. START: **Metro to Nieuwmarkt.**

① ★ **De Waag.** On the fringe of what is now the city's Chinatown, you'll find Amsterdam's only surviving medieval fortified gate. Built in the 14th century, it later became a public weigh house and then a guild house. One of the guilds lodged here was the Surgeon's Guild, immortalized in Rembrandt's painting *The Anatomy Lesson* (1632), which depicts a dissection being conducted in the upper-floor Theatrum Anatomicum. This part of De Waag is rarely open, but you can meander inside the historic ground-floor restaurant (good international fare), In de Waag. ⏱ *15 min. Nieuwmarkt. Metro: Nieuwmarkt.*

② **Amsterdam's Narrowest House.** Walk toward the Dam to

De Waag.

Klein Trippenhuis.

take a look at one of the city's narrowest houses at Oude Hoogstraat 22. The house has a typical Amsterdam bell gable and is only 2m (6½ ft.) wide and 6m (20 ft.) deep. ⏱ *10 min. Oude Hoogstraat 22.*

③ **Klein Trippenhuis.** Nearby you'll find the cornice-gabled Klein Trippenhuis, dubbed "Mr. Trip's Coachman's House." This house is only 2.4m (7¾ ft.) wide. It faces the elegant Trippenhuis at no. 29, which at 22m (72 ft.) is the widest Old Amsterdam house, and was built in 1660 for the wealthy Trip brothers. The story goes that their coachman

Amsterdam's Canal Houses

As you walk around the city's canals, you'll begin to notice that not all canal houses are the same—though they all may look similar. If you look closely, you'll notice a wonderful mix of architectural detail ranging from classical to Renaissance to modern. Most of Amsterdam's 6,800 landmark buildings have gables. These hide the pitched roofs and demonstrate the architect's vertical showmanship in a city where hefty property taxes and expensive canalfront land encouraged pencil-thin buildings.

Canal houses in Amsterdam.

Around 600 old *gevelstenen* (gable stones)—ornamental tiles, sculptures, or reliefs that often play on the original owner's name or profession—remain. Walls in the Begijnhof and on Sint-Luciënsteeg at the **Amsterdam Museum** (p 11) have some good gable stones, including the oldest known (from 1603), showing a milkmaid balancing her buckets.

exclaimed one day: "Oh, if only I could be so lucky as to have a house as wide as my master's door." His master overheard this, and the coachman's wish was granted. The house is now a fashion boutique. ⏱ *10 min. Kloveniersburgwal 26.*

④ Centraal Station. Take a 15-minute walk or jump on any of the trams heading north to Centraal Station, an architectural masterpiece. Designed by architect Petrus Josephus Hubertus Cuypers, it was built between 1884 and 1889 on three artificial islands (supported on 30,000 pilings) in the IJ channel. Amsterdammers thoroughly disliked it at the time. Today, the major transportation hub is an attraction in its own right, partly for its extravagant Dutch neo-Renaissance facade and partly for the liveliness that permanently surrounds it. The left one of

the two central towers has a gilded weathervane; on the right one, there's a clock. Take time to soak up the buzz that swirls around the station in a blur of people, backpacks, bikes, trams, buses, vendors, pickpockets, and junkies. There might even be a street organ—perhaps a century-old Perlee hand-ground barrel-organ, made from richly carved and painted wood. ⏱ *20 min. Tram: 1, 2, 4, 5, 9, 13, 16, 17, 24, 25, or 26 to Centraal Station.*

⑤ Grand Café-Restaurant 1e Klas. Art Nouveau "First Class" (in Dutch, Eerste Klas) was originally a waiting room for first-class rail passengers. Now it's a great place for a drink, a snack, or a full meal, and it's just steps from the trains. *Platform 2B, Centraal Station.* ☎ *020/625-0131. $$.*

6 Museum Het Schip. From Centraal Station, take bus no. 22 heading west (about a 20-min. ride) to the city's most famous example of an Amsterdam School building. The movement's designs, influenced by socialist ideas, can be recognized by a heavy reliance on brickwork, elaborate masonry, painted glass, and wrought-iron work. Of the dozen or so architects who were part of this school, Michel de Klerk (1884–1923) was the most influential. The museum dedicates itself entirely to the architecture of the Amsterdam School, and is housed in a former post office built in 1919 and designed by de Klerk. The post office was only a small part of this large boatlike building (hence its nickname, "the Ship"): It also contained 102 small homes for the working class. The museum features a very interesting exhibit about the Amsterdam School's sources of inspiration. A restored wing originally housed members of a socialist association in the 1920s and provides an intimate view of the Amsterdam School's unique designs. The renovation boasts original woodwork and colors, plus furniture and utensils identical to the ones used in the '20s—even the closets have been restored to their original style. ⏱ 30 min. Spaarndammerplantsoen 140 (at Zaanstraat). ☎ 020/418-2885. www.hetschip.nl. Admission 7.50€ adults, 5€ students. Tues–Sun 11am–5pm. Bus: 22 to Zaanstraat.

7 Scheepvaarthuis. Hop on the bus back to Centraal Station and stay aboard for one stop after the station. Just down Prins Hendrikkade is Maritime House (1916 and 1928)—not to be confused with the nearby **Scheepvaartmuseum** (p 39). This immense turreted fantasy, which originally housed shipping company offices, crawls with incredible bas-reliefs recounting the city's seagoing history. It is the inspired work of Amsterdam School architects Michel de Klerk, Pieter L. Kramer, and J. M. van der Mey, and stands as a monument to Amsterdam School architecture. The ultra-tony Grand Hotel Amrâth Amsterdam now sprawls through the magnificent interior. ⏱ 30 min. Prins Hendrikkade 108. ☎ 020/552-0000. www.amrathamsterdam.com. Tram: All trams to Centraal Station.

8 ARCAM. The Amsterdam Center for Architecture stands on the waterfront a short walk east on Prins Hendrikkade; or board bus no. 22 eastbound for two stops, to Kadijksplein. Its zinc-clad aluminum building (2003), by architect René van Zuuk, is an innovative variation on "blob architecture." Inside, you can take in temporary exhibits on city architecture and tap the center's information resources. ⏱ 30 min. Prins Hendrikkade 600 (on the quay btw. Science Center NEMO and

Museum Het Schip.

The turrets of Scheepvaarthuis.

the Scheepvaartmuseum). ☎ 020/620-4878. www.arcam.nl. Free admission. Tues–Sat 1–5pm. Bus: 22 to Kadijksplein.

9 Lloyd Hotel. Ride the bus back to Centraal Station and connect to tram 26; or walk north and east from ARCAM through the up-and-coming eastern docks area. Leave the tram at Rietlandpark and walk across the park to the renovated building housing the Lloyd Hotel. This Amsterdam School building was constructed in 1917 and served as a "waiting room" after World War I for migrant families heading from Eastern Europe to South America. The ground-floor lobby was a high-ceilinged dining room that would seat 350 immigrants. You can walk around these rooms now and take in the stunning renovation, completed in 2004, that transformed this historical space into an avant-garde hotel (p 130) and dining venue. 🕐 30 min. Oostelijke Handelskade 34 (at Piet Heinkade). ☎ 020/561-3636.

www.lloydhotel.com. Tram: 10 or 26 to Rietlandpark.

10 ★ Panama. Leaving the Lloyd, make a left and walk a few minutes down to the end of the street. Here, you'll find Club Panama, housed in a former power station built around 1899. Today it's one of the city's trendiest venues, with a happening bar, divine restaurant, and celebrated nightclub (p 108). *Oostelijke Handelskade 4 (at Piet Heinkade).* ☎ 020/311-8686. www.panama.nl. Tram: 10 or 26 to Rietlandpark.

11 Panama Restaurant. Wrap up your tour with a drink in the Panama's fantastic loungelike bar while gazing out floor-to-ceiling windows that overlook the river. The bar has a good selection of appetizers and light meals. You can lounge an afternoon or evening away here, watching the preppy after-work crowd sipping on martinis. *Oostelijke Handelskade 4.* ☎ 020/311-8686. $$.

The ARCAM facade.

Amsterdam with Kids

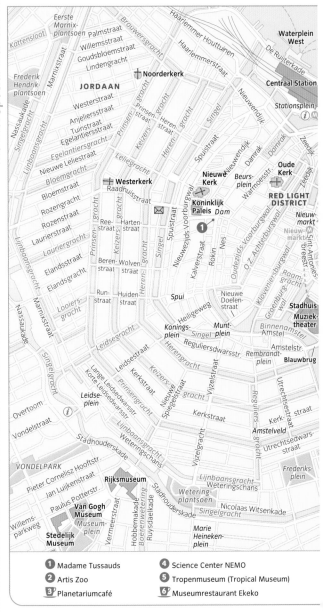

① Madame Tussauds
② Artis Zoo
③ Planetariumcafé
④ Science Center NEMO
⑤ Tropenmuseum (Tropical Museum)
⑥ Museumrestaurant Ekeko

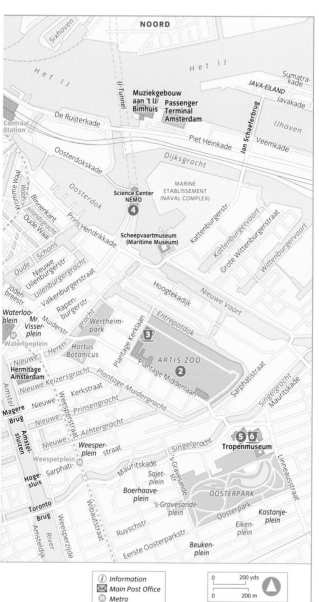

Kids will have plenty to gawk at while walking around Amsterdam—the many houseboats lining the canals and the big barges chugging along the river fascinate children, and a ride on a tram can be an attraction in itself. You'll need to choose from among the suggestions on this tour: Two of them in a day should be enough for most kids. You may also want to take them on the Maritime City tour (later in this chapter), especially if they're over 5. START: **Tram 4, 9, 14, 16, 24, or 25 to the Dam.**

A wax figure of Albert Einstein at Madame Tussauds.

1 ★ **Madame Tussauds.** Spend a frivolous morning at this popular museum. You'll see all the waxen celebrities you'd expect, plus the many hands-on activities that make this museum a winner for kids. In the Be the Next Idol exhibit, modeled after the popular TV show, you sing a tune of your choice and hear what the jury says about you. In the Royalty section, kids can wear tiaras and crowns and have their pictures taken with a wax Queen Beatrix. As you walk around, you'll see celebs from all eras and walks of life, from Charlie Chaplin, Picasso, van Gogh, and Marilyn Monroe to Barack Obama, Nelson Mandela, Lady Gaga, and Harrison Ford as Indiana Jones. Those portrayed are brought to life with memorabilia such as paintings, smoking cigarettes, or pictures of the most memorable moments of their lives. ⏱ *2 hr. Arrive right at opening time to avoid the crowds. Dam 20.* ☎ *020/522-1010. www.madametussauds.nl. Admission 21€ adults, 16€ kids 5–15; purchase tickets online for 2€ less. July–Aug daily 10am–8:30pm; Sept–June daily 10am–5:30pm; open hours may vary (see exceptions on website). Closed Apr 30. Tram: 4, 9, 14, 16, 24, or 25 to the Dam.*

2 ★★★ **Artis Zoo.** Amsterdam's fantastic zoo, established in 1838, is huge—over 14 hectares (35 acres)—so I suggest buying a map at the entrance and targeting the animals your kids want to see most. With one restaurant and three cafes/snack bars to choose from, you can easily spend the whole day here. There are more than 6,000 animals and 1,400 species. You can spot giraffes at the African Savannah and llamas and guanacos in the South American Pampas. Most kids love the chimpanzees; the zoo rotates the animals on display so they—the animals, that is—never seem tired or bored with the visiting throngs. Try to catch one of the daily feedings: Among the interesting ones are the European vultures, sea lions (twice daily), pelicans, and penguins; crocodiles are fed on Sunday only. A list of the current feeding times is available from the Artis office. Included in the admission is entry to Artis's Aquarium, Planetarium, Insect House, and

Kids will love seeing the monkeys at the Artis Zoo.

Geological Museum. There's also a children's farm, where kids can pet assorted small animals. 🕐 *3–5 hr. Plantage Kerklaan 38–40 (at Plantage Middenlaan).* 📞 *0900/278-4796. www.artis.nl. Admission 19€ adults, 18€ seniors, 16€ kids 3–9; you can purchase tickets online. Apr–Oct daily 9am–6pm; Nov–Mar daily 9am–5pm. Tram: 9 or 14 to Plantage Kerklaan.*

3 **Planetariumcafé.** If it's a nice day and you're headed to the zoo, fuel up for your visit by taking a break at this fun eatery inside the planetarium. Fill up on tasty sandwiches and other snacks while looking at the stars and planets. There's also a video arcade. *Inside Artis Zoo Planetarium.* 📞 *0900/278-4796. $.*

4 **★★ Science Center NEMO.** If you find yourself with a rainy afternoon and stir-crazy kids on your hands, head to NEMO. This swooping, modern building, designed by Italian architect Renzo Piano, looks like a graceful oceangoing ship. NEMO is hands-on. It's a great experience for kids 7 or older; and for those ages 4 to 6, who can go through a "Shadow World" especially designed for expanding young minds. Through games, experiments, and demonstrations, kids learn how chain reactions work, search for ETs, blow a soap bubble large enough to stand inside, and much more. Exhibits and experiments in the Wonder Lab answer questions like: How can we use hydrogen as a clean fuel? Why do hormones have the effect they do on teens? The broad, sloping stairway to NEMO's roof is an attraction in itself, a place to hang out and take in the magnificent views. At the top, you are 30m (98 ft.) above the IJ waterway and have sweeping views over the Old Harbor and Eastern Dock. Snacks are served in Café DEK5, which has a grand outdoor terrace, and modest meals in Café Renzo Piano. 🕐 *2 hr. Oosterdok 2 (off Prins Hendrikkade, over the south entrance to the IJ Tunnel).* 📞 *0900/919-1100. www.e-nemo.nl. Admission 13€, free for kids under 4. July–Aug daily 10am–5pm; Sept–June Tues–Sun (and Mon during school vacations) 10am–5pm. Closed Jan 1, Apr 30 & Dec 25. Bus: 22, 42, or 43 to Kadijksplein.*

5 **★ Tropenmuseum (Tropical Museum).** Holland's Royal Institute for the Tropics owns this unusual museum devoted to the study of the cultures of tropical areas around the world. Its focus reflects Holland's former role as a landlord in such countries as Indonesia, Suriname, and the Caribbean islands of (among others) Curaçao, St. Maarten, Bonaire, and Aruba, but the museum has moved far beyond the colonial-era mindset to embrace contemporary issues such as the causes of poverty in the

"A Voice Within Me Is Sobbing"

The handsome merchant house where the Frank family lived faces one of the city's most charming canals. The house was built in 1653 and doubled as a warehouse. Otto Frank, who moved his family here from Frankfurt, Germany, in 1933, stored his herbs and spices in the front of the house. The back of the house (in Dutch, the *Achterhuis*), known as the Secret Annex, later became the family's hiding place. For 25 months, the Frank family (father Otto, his wife Edith, and their two daughters, Margot and Anne) and four family friends hid from Nazi invaders. The hideaway was concealed from the front of the house by a moveable bookcase. Anne began writing in her diary on her birthday, June 12, 1942. Her last entry was on August 1, 1944, shortly before Nazi police raided the hideaway and the family was sent to separate concentration camps. Anne and Margot died of typhus at Bergen-Belsen. Only Otto survived the camps. He returned to the house after the war and fulfilled Anne's wishes to have her diary published. The first edition, in Dutch, appeared in 1947. Since then, Anne's diary has been published in more than 60 languages.

Older kids, especially those who have read *The Diary of Anne Frank,* will be interested in seeing the house where Anne and her family hid for 2 harrowing years. For information on visiting the Anne Frankhuis, see p 9, ❻.

An interactive exhibit at the Science Center NEMO.

developing world and the depletion of the world's tropical rainforests. The building itself is noteworthy for its heavily ornamented 19th-century facade featuring turrets, stepped gables, arched windows, and delicate spires, and a monumental galleried interior court. Of the exhibits, the most fascinating for kids are the walk-through model villages and city-street scenes that capture a moment in daily life. You can stroll through a Nigerian village, an Arab souk, and a traditional yurt tent home of nomads in central Asia. You'll also see fantastic wedding costumes from Thailand and Turkey and bridal jewelry from Northern Sumatra. In Tropenmuseum Junior, kids learn about tropical countries and their people through stories, dances, games, and paintings. This part of the museum is only open to kids ages 6 to 13 (and 1 adult per child). Tropenmuseum Junior is open Wednesday, Saturday, Sunday, national holidays, and during all school holidays. ⏱ *2 hr. Linnaeusstraat 2 (at Mauritskade).* ☎ *020/568-8200. www.tropenmuseum.nl. Admission 9€ adults, 7€ seniors, 5€ students & kids 6–17, 35€ family. Daily 10am–5pm (to 3pm Dec 5, 24 & 31). Closed Jan 1, Apr 30, May 5 & Dec 25. Tram: 7 to Korte 's-Gravesandestraat; 9, 10, or 14 to Alexanderplein.*

6 **Museumrestaurant Ekeko.** Adjacent to Tropenmuseum Junior, this lively cafe is a perfect place to sample food and drinks from one of the tropical countries you've visited. The changing menu might include such specialties as vegetable samosas from India, a Thai beef salad, or Caribbean chicken with rice. *Inside the Tropenmuseum.* ☎ *020/568-8392. $.*

A sculpture from the Tropenmuseum.

Farms for Kids

Children can be amateur farmers for a while at **Geitenboerderij Ridammerhoeve,** Nieuwe Meerlaan 4 (☎ **020/645-5034;** www. geitenboerderij.nl; bus: 170 or 172). They get to feed 150 goats and lambs (along with chickens, a calf or two, and a few potbelly hogs); clean coops and pens; milk a goat; and bottle-feed baby animals. The farm is open Wednesday to Monday from 10am to 5pm; admission is free. At the tiny **Kinderboerderij De Dierencapel,** Bickersgracht 207 (☎ **020/420-6855;** bus: 18, 21, or 22), an urban petting zoo in the Western Islands neighborhood, west of Centraal Station, you'll find endearing piglets, kids (of the goat species), lambs, chickens, ducks, and rabbits; there's a play area too. The petting zoo is open Tuesday to Sunday from 9am to 5pm; admission is free. Equally entertaining is **Kinderboerderij De Pijp,** Lizzy Ansinghstraat 82 (☎ **020/664-8303;** www.kinderboerderijdepijp.nl; tram: 12 or 25), a children's farm off Ferdinand Bolstraat in the De Pijp (the Pipe) urban district south of the center. Here, in addition to the animals mentioned above, kids can get close to donkeys, ponies, peacocks, and turkeys. The farm is open Monday to Friday from 11am to 5pm, and Saturday to Sunday from 1 to 5pm; admission is free.

Maritime Amsterdam

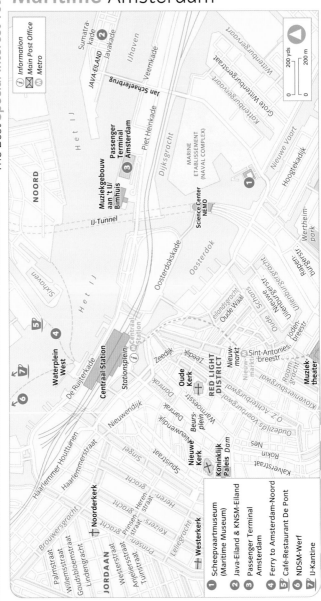

Information
Main Post Office
Metro

0 200 yds
0 200 m

NOORD

Sumatra-kade
Javakade
IJhaven
Veemkade
JAVA-EILAND
Jan Schaeferbrug
Wittenburgervaart
Grote Wittenburgerstraat
Kattenburgervaart
Het IJ

Passenger Terminal Amsterdam

Muziekgebouw aan 't IJ/ Bimhuis

Piet Heinkade
Dijk-gracht
MARINE ETABLISSEMENT (NAVAL COMPLEX)

Nieuwe Vaart
Hoogtekadijk

IJ-Tunnel

Science Center NEMO

Oosterdokskade
Oosterdok
Wertheim-park

Rapen-burgerstr.
burgerstr.
Uilenburgergracht

Sixhaven

Het IJ

Oude Schans
Nieuwe Waal
loden-breestr.

eilandsgracht

Zeedijk
Zeedijk
Nieuw-markt

Sint-Antonies-breestr.

Waterplein West

De Ruijterkade

Centraal Station

Stationsplein
Centraal Station

Oude Kerk

RED LIGHT DISTRICT
Nieuw-markt
Raam-gracht

Muziek-theater

O.Z. Achterburgwal
Oudezijds Voorburgwal
Kloveniersburgwal

Nieuwendijk

Beurs-plein
Damrak
Warmoesstr.

Nieuwe Kerk

Koninklijk Paleis Dam

Nes
Rokin

Kalverstraat

Haarlemmer Houttuinen

Spuistraat

Nieuwendijk

Nieuwezijds Voorburgwal

Singel
Herengracht
Keizersgracht
Prinsengracht
Leliegracht

Westerkerk

Noorderkerk

Brouwersgracht
Palmstraat
Willemsstraat
Goudsbloemstraat
Lindengracht

JORDAAN

Westerstraat
Anjeliersstraat
Tuinstraat

Prinsen- Heren- straat
straat

Westerkerk
Noorderkerk

① Scheepvaartmuseum (Maritime Museum)
② Java-Eiland & KNSM-Eiland
③ Passenger Terminal Amsterdam
④ Ferry to Amsterdam-Noord
⑤ Café-Restaurant De Pont
⑥ NDSM-Werf
⑦ IJ-Kantine

olland's history and culture are inextricably linked to the sea, as you'll discover for yourself on a maritime tour of Amsterdam. This tour takes you to one of the country's best maritime museums, guides you to a redeveloped harbor island and an ultramodern cruise liner dock, and sails you around the ship channel by ferry. START: **Bus 22, 42, or 43 to Kattenburgerplein.**

Scheepvaartmuseum (Maritime Museum).

1 ★★ kids **Scheepvaartmuseum (Maritime Museum).** This gem of a museum overlooking the busy Oosterdok (Eastern Dock) reopened in September 2011 after being closed for more than 2 years for major renovations. Inside the grand museum, highlights include the Royal Barge, used by the monarchy from 1818 to 1982. The rooms are filled with boats and ship models; paintings and prints of ships, seascapes, navigational instruments, cannons and other weaponry; old maps and charts; and important historical papers. Moored alongside is a full-size replica of the United East India Company (V.O.C.) merchant ship *Amsterdam,* which foundered off Hastings, England, in 1749 on its maiden voyage to the East Indies (Indonesia). Climb aboard and

explore every nook and cranny. Reenactors create scenes from everyday life on the ship. Sailors fire cannons, sing sea shanties, mop the deck, hoist cargo on board, and attend a solemn "burial at sea." You can watch sailmakers and rope makers at work and see the cook prepare a shipboard meal in the galley. ⏲ *3 hr. Kattenburgerplein 1 (off Prins Hendrikkade).* ☎ *020/523-2222. www. scheepvaartmuseum.nl. The following prices and hours were current when the museum was last open and are likely to change. Admission 7.50€ adults, 4€ kids 6–17. Tues–Sat 10am–5pm (also Mon during school vacations); Sun noon–5pm. Bus: 22, 42, or 43 to Kadijksplein.*

2 **Java-Eiland & KNSM-Eiland.** These two man-made islands, joined

Java-Eiland and KNSM-Eiland are filled with modern residential buildings.

together to form one long island, were once thickly strewn with harbor warehouses and other port installations. Now, Java island and KNSM island comprise a shiny modern residential zone, affording an indication of where Amsterdam is headed in the 21st century. The best thing you can do here is to stroll up

The Passenger Terminal Amsterdam.

and down the island, perusing the vast apartment complexes, until your interest or energy, or both, run out. 🕘 *30 min. IJhaven. Tram: 10 to Azartplein (or take tram 26 to Rietlandpark, and transfer to 10).*

3 kids Passenger Terminal Amsterdam. It can be interesting to visit this ultramodern facility just east of Centraal Station when a giant oceangoing cruise liner is tied up at the dock on Het IJ ship channel. At other times, you might have to make do with a Rhine River cruise boat down from Switzerland or Germany. The neighboring building on the wharf is the shiny glass concert hall Muziekgebouw aan 't IJ (p 117). 🕘 *30 min. Piet Heinkade 27. ☎ 020/ 509-1000. www.ptamsterdam.nl. Open when a cruise ship is moored. Free admission. Tram: 25 or 26 to Passenger Terminal Amsterdam.*

4 ★ kids Ferry to Amsterdam-Noord. To view the city's busy harbor traffic up close, take the free 5-minute ride on the Buiksloterweg-veer (Buiksloterweg Ferry) from the Waterplein West dock behind Centraal Station across to the north bank of Het IJ waterway. There's not a lot you can see in this northern district of Amsterdam without a bicycle, or time enough to shuttle around by bus (there's no tram or Metro service in Noord). I suggest you just kick around on the north shore for a short time. The EYE Film Instituut (www.eyefilm.nl; p 118), the city's film museum and art-house cinema, is due to move here in 2012 from its classic old home in Vondelpark. ⏱ *20 min. Ferry: Buiksloterwegveer.*

5️⃣ Café-Restaurant De Pont.

This eatery on the north bank is a great place to while away some time. Have a coffee and a snack in its cafe or dine on a full meal in the Continental restaurant, while enjoying the great waterfront views. *Buiksloterweg 3–5 (at the ferry dock).* ☎ *020/636-3388. $$.*

6️⃣ ★ kids NDSM-Werf. Board the

free NDSM-Werfveer (NDSM Wharf Ferry) from behind Centraal Station to the NDSM Wharf. This former facility of the Nederlandsche Dok en Scheepsbouw Maatschappij (Netherlands Dock and Shipyard Corporation) was used for shipbuilding, dry-docking, and ship repair. Now in the process of large-scale redevelopment, the wharf is an expanding star

on the city's cultural scene, providing a home for performance venues, and art and design studios. Here, too, is the **Amstel Botel** (p 126), the city's only floating hotel. Within easy torpedo range of this waterborne lodging, a rusting, 1950s-vintage ex-Soviet Navy Zulu class attack submarine is tied up at an offshore wharf. Greenpeace International's retired environmental warrior of the seas, *Sirius,* is berthed across the dock from the Amstel Botel. And the **Pannenkoekenboot (Pancake Boat;** ☎ 020/636-8817; www. pannenkoekenboot.nl), sorties from here to prowl the harbor laden with pancake-munching kids and shang-haied parents. ⏱ *1 hr. Ferry: NDSM-Werfveer.*

7️⃣ ★ IJ-Kantine. Even if "IJ Can-

teen" hasn't much allure as a name, the reality behind the handle is far superior. This large, multifaceted cafe, brasserie, and restaurant on the NDSM Wharf does indeed occupy the former shipyard's cafeteria, restored to a squared-away shine, and it sports a grand waterside terrace. *MT Ondinaweg 15–17 (at the ferry dock).* ☎ *020/633-7162. $$.*

The free NDSM Wharf Ferry.

Alternative Amsterdam

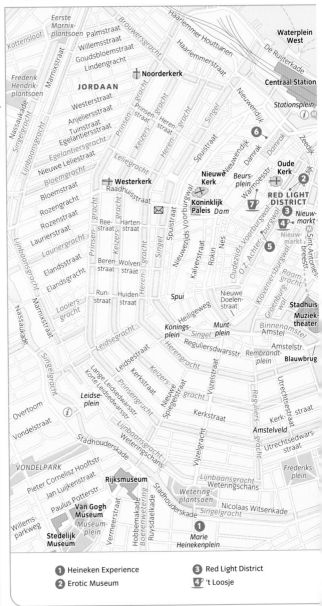

- **1** Heineken Experience
- **2** Erotic Museum
- **3** Red Light District
- **4** 't Loosje

NOORD

Sixhaven

Het IJ

Het IJ

JAVA-EILAND

| 0 | 200 yds |
| 0 | 200 m |

i Information
✉ Main Post Office
Ⓜ Metro

De Ruijterkade

IJ-Tunnel

Muziekgebouw
aan 't IJ/
Bimhuis

Passenger
Terminal
Amsterdam

Jan Schaeferbrug

IJhaven

Centraal
Station

Piet Heinkade

Veemkade

Oosterdokskade

Dijksgracht

Kromme Waal

Wijde
Binnenkant
Eilandsgracht
Oude Waal

Oosterdok

Prins Hendrikkade

Science Center
NEMO

MARINE
ETABLISSEMENT
(NAVAL COMPLEX)

Kattenburgerstr.

Kattenburgervaart

Grote Wittenburgerstraat

Wittenburgervaart

Scheepvaartmuseum
(Maritime Museum)

Oude
Nieuwe
Uilenburgerstr.

Schans

Nieuwe
Uilenburgergracht

Joden-
breestr.

Valkenburgerstraat

Hoogtekadijk

Nieuwe Vaart

Rapen-
burgerstr.

-gracht

Entrepotdok

Entrepotdok

Waterloo-
plein

Ⓜ Waterlooplein

Mr.
Visser-
plein

Muiderstr.

Wertheim-
park

Plantage Kerklaan

ARTIS ZOO

Heren-

Nieuwe

Hortus
Botanicus

Plantage Middenlaan

Sarphatistraat

Hermitage
Amsterdam

Nieuwe Keizersgracht

Kerkstraat

Plantage Muidergracht

Singelgracht
Mauritskade

Amstel

Magere
Brug

Nieuwe Prinsengracht

Nieuwe Weesperstraat

Achtergracht

Amstel-
sluizen

Nieuwe
Weesper-
plein
straat

Singelgracht

Tropenmuseum

Weesperplein

Mauritskade

Sajet-
plein

'sGravesande-
str.

Hoge-
sluis

Sarphati-

Boerhaave-
plein

OOSTERPARK

Linnaeusstraat

Toronto
Brug

Weesperzijde

Wibautstraat

'sGravesande-
plein

Oosterpark

Eiken-
plein

Kastanje-
plein

Amsteldijk

River

Ruyschstr.

Eerste Oosterparkstr.

Beuken-
plein

❺ Hash Marihuana & Hemp Museum

❻ Sexmuseum Amsterdam

❼ Winston Club

Amsterdam has a reputation for being a wild party town with tolerant attitudes toward many aspects of life. It tolerates the growing and selling of cannabis in small amounts, and Dutch law allows prostitution. The Red Light District is known the world over for its scantily clad women luring customers from behind glass windows. This tour will give you a chance to discover the wilder side of Amsterdam, but not surprisingly, your day may not end until well after midnight. START: **Tram 16 or 24 to Stadhouderskade.**

❶ ★ Heineken Experience.

This place is usually a hit with 20-somethings, who enjoy the two free beers as much as they enjoy the myriad rides and shows. It's a hoot if you just get loose and go with the flow—and you'll learn a few things about beer while you're at it. It's housed inside the former working brewery (built ca. 1867). The operation moved out of this facility in 1988, but a minibrewery opened in 2008 to afford a miniview of how brewing works. The old fermentation tanks, each capable of holding a million glasses of Heineken, are still here, along with the multistory malt silos, all manner of vintage

Visitors examine a copper brewing kettle at the Heineken Experience.

brewing equipment and implements, and a stable for the strapping Shire horses that pull Heineken's old-world promotional drays. ⏲ *2 hr. Stadhouderskade 78 (at Ferdinand Bolstraat).* ☎ *020/ 523-9435. www.heinekenexperience. com. Admission 15€ (includes 2 beers); kids 1–15 1€ per year of age, up to a maximum 12€; beverages containing alcohol not permitted for kids under 16; online ticket purchase available. Daily 11am–7pm. Closed Jan 1, Apr 30 & Dec 25–26. Tram: 16 or 24 to Stadhouderskade.*

❷ Erotic Museum.

Spread over five floors, this wacky place boasts many provocative prints and drawings, including some by John Lennon, along with latex mannekins. More interesting is a re-creation of a red-light window, an extensively equipped S&M playroom, Kama Sutra-style Indian carvings, and erotic antiques. Don't miss the X-rated cartoon depicting some of the things Snow White apparently got up to with the Seven Dwarfs that we were never told about as kids! ⏲ *45 min. Oudezijds Achterburgwal 54.* ☎ *020/623-1834. Admission 5€. Sun–Thurs 11am– 1am; Fri–Sat 11am–2am. Tram: 4, 9, 14, 16, 24, or 25 to the Dam.*

❸ Red Light District.

Upon leaving the Erotic Museum, you'll find yourself in Amsterdam's infamous Rosse Buurt (Red Light District). If you take a peek down any of the tiny alleyways, you'll see the prostitutes hanging out behind their windows, waiting for customers. Some may be on cellphones, some may be knitting. Many will be in various stages of undress (though never fully naked). If the curtains are closed, then you know that a deal has been . . . consummated. Probably what you'll notice most of all are the throngs of testosterone-driven men circling these tiny alleyways with hungry eyes. It isn't dangerous here, just a bit seedy, though you shouldn't take photos at any time; it's best to hide your camera when you stroll here, especially at night. Early evening is the best time to visit, before it gets crowded but late enough that you can see the red lights reflecting off the canals. ⏱ *30 min. Along Oudezijds Achterburgwal and the tiny alleyways that intersect it. Metro: Nieuwmarkt.*

An exhibit from the Erotic Museum.

In the Red Light District, you'll find sex shops, live sex shows, and prostitutes waiting for customers behind windows.

🄴 **'t Loosje.** Steps from the Red Light District (toward Nieuwmarkt) is a busy, friendly cafe that was built in 1900. Tiles from that period still ornament the walls. It's a great place to people-watch. Many beers are on tap, and they have a good choice of snacks. Try the Dutch croquettes or bitterballen (fried minced-meat-and-potato balls) dipped in hot mustard. *Nieuwmarkt 32–34.* ☎ *020/627-2635. $.*

🄵 ★ **Hash Marihuana & Hemp Museum.** Only in Amsterdam, eh? This museum in the Red Light District will teach you everything you wanted to know about hash, marijuana, and related products. The museum does not promote drug use; instead it aims to make you better informed. There's a cannabis garden where you can see plants at various stages of development. Some exhibits shed light on the medicinal use of cannabis and on hemp's past and present-day uses as a natural fiber. Among several

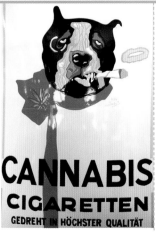

A display from the Hash Marihuana & Hemp Museum.

notable artworks is David Teniers the Younger's painting *Hemp-Smoking Peasants in a Smoke House* (1660). ⏱ 1 hr. Oudezijds Achterburgwal 148 (off Damstraat). ☎ 020/624-8926. www.hashmuseum.com. Admission 9€ adults, free for kids under 13 (must be accompanied by an adult). Daily 10am–11pm. Closed Apr 30. Tram: 4, 9, 14, 16, 24, or 25 to the Dam.

6 Sexmuseum Amsterdam. For more of Amsterdam's wild side, head over to this museum—or "Venustempel," as it dubs itself. More than half a million visitors traipse through here every year to learn more about the history of sex. Teenagers end up giggling quite a bit. "Sex through the ages and cultures" is the theme of one exhibit, which includes such 19th-century erotic objects as a fragment of a Delft blue tile showing a man with an erection playing cards. There's an interesting exhibit about early erotic photography and many erotic prints and drawings and trinkets decorated with naughty pictures. It's open late, so you can come here after dark, before you head out to the club below. ⏱ 1 hr. Damrak 18 (near Centraal Station). ☎ 020/622-8376. www.sexmuseumamsterdam.com. Admission 4€; under 17 not admitted. Daily 9:30am–11:30pm. Closed Dec 25. Tram: 1, 2, 4, 5, 9, 13, 16, 17, 24, 25, or 26 to Centraal Station.

7 ★ Winston Club. End your day at this very happening and fun venue inside the Winston Hotel at the edge of the Red Light District (see p 109 for the Nightlife listing). There are light snacks and drinks. *Winston Hotel, Warmoesstraat 129 (behind Beursplein).* ☎ 020/623-1380. $. ●

A display from the Sexmuseum Amsterdam.

Golden Age **Canals**

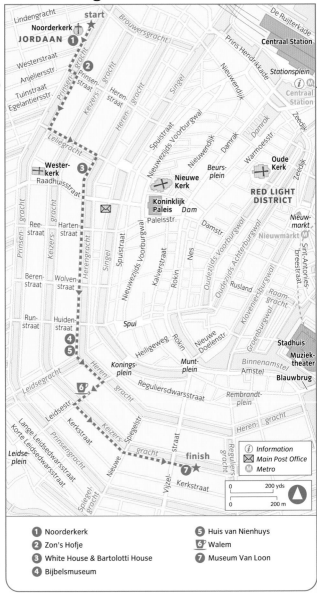

1 Noorderkerk
2 Zon's Hofje
3 White House & Bartolotti House
4 Bijbelsmuseum
5 Huis van Nienhuys
6 Walem
7 Museum Van Loon

Previous page: Biking in the Jordaan neighborhood.

Amsterdam's glory days date to the 17th century, a time known as the "Golden Age." This tour gives you an in-depth view of the awesome architecture of that time. You pass innumerable canal houses with gables in various styles (bell, step, neck, and variations), and peek into hidden almshouses—these are like cloisters with a courtyard garden, and are great places for a moment of rest and contemplation. In addition, you'll visit two small but fascinating museums. START: Tram: 1, 2, 5, 13, or 17 to Martelaarsgracht.

① ★ **Noorderkerk.** The North Church was the last masterpiece by celeb architect of the time, Hendrick de Keyser, the guiding hand behind many of Amsterdam's historic churches. Dating to 1623, it was built for the poor Calvinist faithful of the Jordaan district. It was restored during the 1990s and today has an active congregation. From November to April, a 1-hour classical-music recital takes place here every Saturday at 2pm. Also on Saturdays, I love to browse the farmers market (10am–3pm) with organic products, on Noordermarkt, the square on which the church stands. ⏱ *20 min. Noordermarkt 44–48 (at Prinsengracht & Lindenstraat). Church:* ☎ *020/ 626-6436. www.noorderkerk.org. Free*

Noorderkerk.

admission. Mon 10:30am–12:30pm; Sat 11am–1pm; Sun services 10am & 7pm. Recitals: ☎ *020/620-4415. www. noorderkerkconcerten.nl. Admission 15€ adults, 5€ kids 12 and under.*

② **Zon's Hofje.** Walk up Prinsengracht to no. 159, where you'll find a hidden *hofje* (almshouse) surrounding a courtyard garden at the end of a long passageway. Almshouses were built by wealthy citizens starting in the 14th century for the old and needy; many were inhabited by pious women. Today, students, seniors, and people who need assisted living reside in almshouses. At Zon's Hofje, the outer door is open from 10am to 5pm Monday through Saturday, and you can walk quietly through the passageway to the serene courtyard. The city's Mennonites once held meetings in this courtyard, which they called *De Kleine Zon* (the Little Sun). *Prinsengracht 159–171.*

③ **The White House & the Bartolotti House.** Back on Prinsengracht, turn left along the picturesque Leliegracht canal, then right onto Herengracht, the ultimate Amsterdam canal address for flourishing bankers and merchants in the 17th century. At no. 168 is a building known as Het Witte Huijs (the White House) for its whitish-gray, neoclassical sandstone facade. This graceful house was built in 1638 for Michiel Pauw, who established a short-lived trading colony in America at Hoboken, New Jersey. The flamboyant Huis Bartolotti (Bartolotti House) next door (nos. 170–172), from 1621, was built for Guillielmo

The Bartolotti House.

Bartolotti, who began life as Willem van den Heuvel and switched to the fancier moniker after he made a bundle in brewing and banking. It likely was designed by architect Hendrick de Keyser. *Herengracht 168–172.*

4 ★ **Bijbels Museum (Biblical Museum).** Stroll down Herengracht, taking in the view of the canals and canal houses with their varied gables. Two of a group of four 1660s houses (nos. 364–370) with delicate neck gables house the Biblical Museum. The houses were designed by architect Philips Vingboons for timber merchant Jacob Cromhout, and are known as the Cromhouthuizen or as the "Father, Mother, and Twins." The

An exhibit from the Bijbels Museum (Biblical Museum).

museum itself features Bibles and things biblical, but its canal-house setting with its elegant stucco decoration, dizzying elliptical staircase, and illuminated ceilings (1718) by Jacob de Wit, depicting scenes from Roman mythology, are worth the admission price alone. ⏱ *1 hr. Herengracht 366–368.* ☎ *020/624-2436. www.bijbelsmuseum.nl. Admission 8€ adults, 4.75€ students, 4€ kids 13–17. Mon–Sat 10am–5pm; Sun & holidays 11am–5pm. Closed Jan 1 & Apr 30.*

5 **Huis van Nienhuys.** A few steps down Herengracht bring you to this princely residence (at nos. 380–382). Constructed in 1890 for tobacco merchant Jacob Nienhuys, the mansion now houses the Netherlands Institute for War Documentation. On the opposite bank of Herengracht is the tiny Beulingsluis, a connecting canal with a rare view of houses standing directly in the water. If you cross over for a close-up look, take in the stone cat on the facade at Herengracht 395, stalking a carved mouse on the house across Beulingsluis at no. 397. Back at Huis van Nienhuys, continue across elegant Leidsegracht (dug in 1664 for barge traffic) and walk along Leidsestraat to its junction with Keizersgracht. *Herengracht 380–382.*

6 ★ **Walem.** Along with an interior designed by Philippe Starck, this trendy cafe-restaurant has two fine terraces (one outside beside the canal and the other at the rear in a sheltered and quiet garden patio). The Mediterranean-style sandwiches and salads make for a great lunch. *Keizersgracht 449 (at Leidsestraat).* ☎ *020/625-3544. $$.*

7 ★ **Museum Van Loon.** Continue down Keizersgracht to yet another magnificent canal house, this one dating to 1672. Its first occupant was the artist Ferdinand Bol, a student of Rembrandt. The elegant home was owned by the Van Loon family from 1884 to 1945. On its walls hang more than 80 family portraits, including those of Willem van Loon, one of the founders of the Dutch United East India Company. A marble staircase with an ornately curlicued brass balustrade leads up through the house, connecting restored period rooms that are filled with richly decorated

The exquisite garden of the Museum Van Loon.

paneling, stuccowork, mirrors, fireplaces, furnishings, porcelain, medallions, chandeliers, rugs, and more. Be sure to look out into the garden at the carefully tended hedges and the coach house modeled on a Greek temple. ⏱ *1 hr. Keizersgracht 672.* ☎ *020/624-5255. www.museumvanloon.nl. Admission 8€ adults, 6€ students, 4€ kids 6–18. Wed–Mon 11am–5pm. Closed Jan 1, Apr 30 & Dec 25.*

Gables 101

Most of Amsterdam's 6,800 landmark buildings have gables. These hide the pitched roofs and demonstrate the architect's vertical showmanship in a city where hefty property taxes and expensive canalfront land encouraged pencil-thin buildings. If you can pick out Amsterdam's various gable styles without developing Sistine Chapel–neck syndrome, you can date the buildings fairly accurately. Of the earliest, triangular wood gables (1250–1550) only two remain, at no. 34 in the Begijnhof and at Zeedijk 1. Later developments in stone on this theme (1600–50) were the pointy spout gable and the step gable, which, as the name suggests, looks like a series of steps. The graceful neck gable (1640–1790) looks like a headless neck, with curlicues on the shoulders.

Incidentally, the *hijsbalk*—the hook you see on many gables—might look to be ideal for a hanging, but is actually used with rope and pulley for hauling large, heavy items in and out of homes that have steep, narrow staircases.

The Jordaan

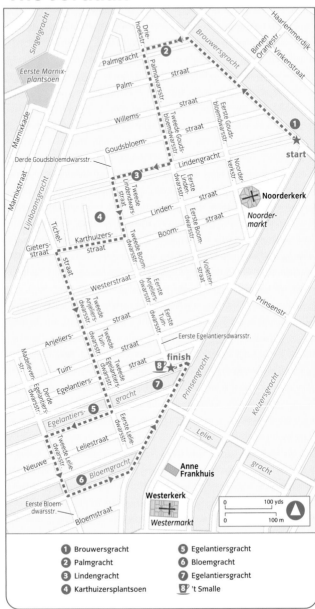

1 Brouwersgracht
2 Palmgracht
3 Lindengracht
4 Karthuizersplantsoen
5 Egelantiersgracht
6 Bloemgracht
7 Egelantiersgracht
8 't Smalle

The Jordaan is one of Amsterdam's most interesting neighborhoods, where many of the city's more successful artists, intellectuals, and slightly older yuppies reside. Among the district's charms are tiny canals with many bridges, and several of the delightful, centuries-old almshouses called *hofjes*. If you enter these courtyards, tread softly—people live here. This walk can be taken at any time, though the late afternoon on a warm day would be best so you can end at a canalside cafe. START: **Tram 1, 2, 4, 5, 9, 16, 24, 25, or 26 to Centraal Station, then a 10-minute walk to Brouwersgracht.**

① ★ **Brouwersgracht.** Stroll along this old houseboat-lined canal and cross Lindengracht. You'll pass a bronze sculpture from 1979 of Jordaan schoolchild Kees de Jongen, a popular fictional character of Dutch writer Theo Thijssen (1879–1943). Keep going until you cross Willemsstraat, then look across the water for a wide view of the modern De Blauwe Burgt apartment block. (You can cross over on the Oranjebrug bridge for a close-up look.) It's a good example of new architecture mixed with the old.

② **Palmgracht.** Turn left onto this tree-shaded street, which was once a canal. The house at nos. 28–38 hides a small cobblestone courtyard garden behind an orange door that's the entrance to the Raepenhofje, an

Palmgracht.

almshouse from 1648. If you're lucky, the door will be open and you can peek into the courtyard. *Palmgracht 28–38.*

③ **Lindengracht.** Turn left on Palmdwarsstraat and cross over Willemsstraat (which used to be a canal known as Goudsbloemgracht) onto Tweede Goudsbloemdwarsstraat. Cross over Goudsbloemstraat to Lindengracht. This was once the Jordaan's most important canal—since filled in—and is now the scene of a lively Saturday street market. The 15 small houses (originally there were 19) of the pretty Suyckerhoff Hofje (or Suyckerhofje), at Lindengracht 149–163, were built in 1670

Brouwersgracht canal is lined with houseboats.

An outdoor cafe in Lindengracht.

as a refuge for Protestant widows and for women of good moral standing and a "tranquil character," who had been abandoned by their husbands. The door may be closed but you can generally open it during daylight hours and walk along the narrow entrance corridor to a courtyard garden filled with flowers and plants. *Lindengracht 149–163*.

4 Karthuizersplantsoen. From Lindengracht, turn left onto Tweede Lindendwarsstraat. Nothing is left of the Carthusian monastery from 1394 that once stretched from here to Lijnbaansgracht and that was destroyed in the 1570s. A playground marks the spot where its cemetery stood. At Karthuizersstraat 11–19 is a row of neck-gabled houses from 1737, named after the four seasons: Lente, Zomer, Herfst, and Winter (spring, summer, fall, winter). Next door (despite the unusual numbering), at nos. 69–191, is the Huyszitten-Weduwenhof, which dates from 1650 and used to shelter poor widows. Today students live in these houses, which surround a large interior courtyard. *Karthuizersstraat 11–19*.

5 ★ Egelantiersgracht. Hang a left on Tichelstraat to reach Egelantiersgracht. As you make your way here, you'll notice the tall spire of the Westerkerk. Named for the eglantine rose, or sweetbrier, Egelantiersgracht is one of the city's most picturesque and tranquil small canals and is lined with 17th- and 18th-century houses. This is where successful Amsterdam artisans lived in the 17th century. If the door is open, take a peek into the Andrieshofje at nos. 107–145. Cattle

Egelantiersgracht.

Bloemgracht.

farmer Ivo Gerrittsszoon financed this almshouse of 36 houses, which was completed in 1617 and remodeled in 1884. A corridor decorated with Delft blue tiles leads up to a small courtyard with a manicured garden. *Egelantiersgracht 107–145.*

⑥ **Bloemgracht.** The grandest of the Jordaan canals, Bloemgracht originally was home to workers who produced dyes and paints. The three fine step-gabled houses at nos. 87–91 date from 1642, and are now owned by the Hendrick de Keyser Foundation, an organization that preserves buildings of architectural and historic importance throughout Holland. Their carved gable stones represent a townsman, a countryman, and a seaman. Nos. 77 and 81 are two former sugar refineries from 1752 and 1763, respectively.

⑦ ★ **Egelantiersgracht.** Make a left on Prinsengracht and you'll find yourself back at Egelantiersgracht. The hardware store at nos. 2–6, at the corner of Prinsengracht, is a fine example of Amsterdam School architecture design from 1917. Its intricate brickwork and cast-iron ornaments were influenced by Art Nouveau. (See "Architectural Amsterdam," p 26, for more examples of this influential local style.) To

the left of the store, at no. 8, a step-gabled house from 1649 is decorated with sandstone ornaments and gable stones that depict the English monk St. Willibrord (the first bishop of Utrecht, in 695) and a brewer.

⑧ ★ **'t Smalle.** With its waterside terrace, this cafe is one of the best in the Jordaan for a drink and a typical Dutch snack of *bitterballen* (fried minced-meat-and-potato balls), chunks of Gouda dipped in mustard, or homemade pea soup. *Egelantiersgracht 12 (at Prinsengracht).* ☎ *020/623-9617. $.*

Walking Tour Tips

Allow between 2 and 2½ hours for walking around the Jordaan. If you want to visit one of this neighborhood's lively markets, go either on a Monday morning or on Saturday. On Monday, there's a flea market on Noordermarkt and a textiles market on Westerstraat where you find, among other items, fabrics, and secondhand clothing. On Saturday, Noordermarkt hosts a bird market and a farmers market that has organically grown produce, and Lindengracht has a general street market. For more on shopping in this area, see chapter 4.

The Jewish Quarter

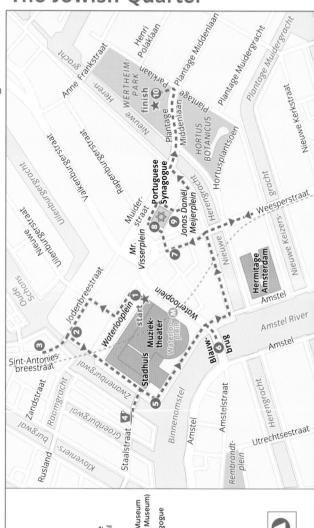

1 Waterlooplein
Flea Market

2 Museum Het
Rembrandthuis

3 Huis De Pinto

4 Puccini

5 Jewish Resistance
Fighters Memorial

6 Blauwbrug

7 Joods Historisch Museum
(Jewish Historical Museum)

8 Portuguese Synagogue

9 The Dockworker

10 Wertheimpark

--- Metro

0   100 yds
0   100 m

This historical area, just to the east of the Old Center, used to be Amsterdam's main Jewish neighborhood. It has changed almost beyond recognition since World War II, but there remain mementos and memorials of Amsterdam's once-thriving Jewish community. It's a great area for a stroll. START: **Tram 9 or 14 to Waterlooplein.**

Waterlooplein Flea Market.

① ★ Waterlooplein Flea Market. The most popular flea market in Amsterdam sells everything from sweaters, hats, and gloves to CDs, books, and faux Rembrandt paintings. You'll also find stalls selling raw herring and herring sandwiches. If you're feeling adventurous, try a local favorite: a herring sandwich with pickles and raw onion. In the passageway between the Muziektheater (the home of the Netherlands Opera and Ballet) and the Town Hall, you'll see three columns filled with water. This is the NAP, the *Normaal Amsterdams Peil* (Amsterdam Ordnance Datum), a fixed point against which sea level measurements are made. *Waterlooplein. Market open Mon–Sat 10am–5pm.*

② ★★ Museum Het Rembrandthuis. Continue down on Waterlooplein to the end and turn left on Jodenbreestraat (Broad St. of the Jews). At nos. 4–6, you'll find Rembrandt's house, now a fabulously preserved museum. Although Rembrandt was not Jewish, he often painted portraits of his Jewish friends and neighbors. A visit to the museum will not only give you an insight into the artist's life and work, but will also give you an opportunity to see the interior and furnishings of a 17th-century home in this area. The house was constructed in 1606; Rembrandt bought it in 1639 and lived here until he went bankrupt in 1658. *See p 19,* ⑦.

③ Huis De Pinto. Cross over the Sint-Antoniesluis bridge at the western end of Jodenbreestraat, and take a moment to enjoy the views up and down the canal. Walk a little way along Sint-Antoniesbreestraat, to no. 69, to view the magnificent De Pinto House. The mansion dates from the early 17th century. In 1651, it came into the possession of the Jewish businessman and scholar Isaäc de Pinto, and later in the century was remodeled in the ornate Italian Renaissance style. *Sint-Antoniesbreestraat 69.*

A room in the Museum Het Rembrandthuis.

The Blauwbrug (Blue Bridge).

4 Puccini. Just across the bridge over the Zwanenburgwal canal to Staalstraat, you'll find this delightful cafe—a great spot for brunch or lunch—that makes luscious pastries and tarts, and savory sandwiches. *Staalstraat 21 (at Waterlooplein).* ☎ *020/620-8458. $.*

5 Jewish Resistance Fighters Memorial. Retrace your steps across the bridge and turn right to see this striking black marble monument. It's dedicated to those Jews who tried to resist Nazi oppression and to the people who helped them. *Waterlooplein.*

The Jewish Resistance Fighters Memorial.

6 Blauwbrug (Blue Bridge). Turn left at the monument (the Amstel River will be to your right) and walk toward this cast-iron bridge with its blue lanterns. The bridge, inspired by Paris's Pont Alexandre III and opened in 1884, is named after a 16th-century timber bridge painted blue after the 1578 Protestant take-over of the city. Impressionist artist George Hendrik Breitner (1857–1923) painted a picture of this bridge in the 1880s. *Amstelstraat–Waterlooplein.*

7 ★★ Joods Historisch Museum (Jewish Historical Museum). Don't cross the Blauw-brug; instead, continue straight ahead, keeping the river to your right, and go left on Nieuwe Herengracht. Walk along the canal—a picture-perfect outlook of canal houses and house-boats—to the next bridge, and turn left. The building that holds the Jew-ish Historical Museum once housed four synagogues built by Jewish refu-gees from Germany and Poland in the 17th and 18th centuries. They survived the Nazi occupation of Amsterdam during World War II more or less intact, and in 1987 they became home to an impressive collection of Jewish paintings and decorative and cere-monial objects that were looted dur-ing the war. In addition to admiring the buildings themselves (which include the oldest public synagogue in Europe), you can enjoy some short documentaries about Jewish customs and traditions. The museum cafe is a great place to have a cup of coffee and a pastry, or a light kosher meal. ⏱ 1½ hr. Nieuwe Amstelstraat 1. ☎ 020/531-0310. www.jhm.nl. *Admission 9€ adults, 6€ seniors & students, 4.50€ kids 13–17; combined admission with Portuguese Synagogue 12€ adults, 11€ seniors & students, 8.50€ kids 13–17. Daily 11am–5pm. Closed Jewish New Year (2 days).*

8 ★ Portuguese Synagogue. Across the street from the museum

An exhibit from the Jewish Historical Museum.

stands this synagogue (1675), modeled on the Temple in Jerusalem and raised by Sephardic Jews from Spain and Portugal. The building was restored in the 1950s, and today it looks essentially as it did 3 centuries ago, with the women's gallery supported by 12 stone columns to represent the Twelve Tribes of Israel, and the large, low-hanging brass chandeliers that together hold 1,000 candles. 🕐 *30 min. Mr. Visserplein 3.* ☎ *020/624-5351. www.portugese synagoge.nl. Admission 6.50€ adults, 5€ seniors & students, 4€ kids 13–17; combined admission with Jewish Historical Museum 12€ adults, 11€ seniors & students, 8.50€ kids 13–17. Apr–Oct Sun–Fri 10am–4pm; Nov–Mar Sun–Thurs 10am–4pm, Fri 10am–2pm. Closed for visits on Jewish holidays.*

⑨ *The Dockworker.* Jonas Daniël Meijerplein is where many Jews were forced to wait for their deportation to concentration camps. This bronze statue by Mari Andriessen was erected in 1952 in commemoration of the February 1941 strike by the workers of Amsterdam to protest the deportation of the city's Jewish population. The strike, one of the biggest collective actions in all of occupied Europe against the Nazi persecution, was violently suppressed. *Jonas Daniël Meijerplein.*

⑩ Wertheim Park. At the center of this small park is a memorial (1993) by sculptor Jan Wolkers to the victims of Auschwitz. Six large "broken" mirrors laid flat on the ground reflect a shattered sky and cover a buried urn containing ashes of the dead from the concentration camp. NOOIT MEER AUSCHWITZ (NEVER AGAIN AUSCHWITZ) reads the dedication. An information board lists in impersonal round numbers some of the gruesome statistics of the Holocaust: Of 140,000 members of Holland's Jewish community, 107,000 were deported to concentration camps, and just 5,200 returned; of the 95,000 sent to Auschwitz and Sobibor, fewer than 500 survived. One of those who perished (at Bergen-Belsen) was Anne Frank, who has a street named after her at the far end of the park. *Plantage Middenlaan.*

The interior of the Portuguese Synagogue.

The Old Center

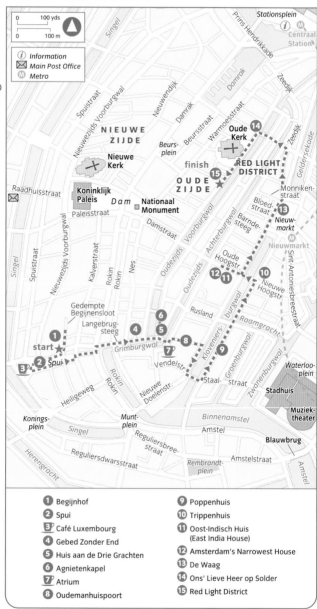

0   100 yds
0   100 m

(i) Information
✉ Main Post Office
Ⓜ Metro

Stationsplein
Prins Hendrikkade
(i)
Ⓜ Centraal Station

Singel
Spuistraat
Nieuwezijds Voorburgwal
Nieuwendijk
Damrak
Beursstraat
Warmoesstraat
Zeedijk
Zeedijk
Gelderskade

NIEUWE ZIJDE

Beurs-plein

Nieuwe Kerk

finish

Oude Kerk **14**

RED LIGHT DISTRICT

OUDE ZIJDE

15 ★

Raadhuisstraat
✉

Koninklijk Paleis

Dam ■ Nationaal Monument

Paleisstraat

Damstraat

Oudezijds Voorburgwal
Achterburgwal
Barnde-steeg

Monniken-straat

Bloed-straat **13**

Nieuw-markt

Ⓜ Nieuwmarkt

Sint Antoniesbreestraat

Singel
Spuistraat
Nieuwezijds Voorburgwal
Kalverstraat
Rokin
Rokin
Nes

Damstraat

Oudezijds Voorburgwal
Oudezijds

Oude Hoogstr. **12 11**

Nieuwe Hoogstr. **10**

burgwal

Rusland

Raamgracht

Gedempte Begijnensloot
Langebrug-steeg

6
4 5
8

1
start ★

2 Spui
3'

Grimburgwal

7

Vendelstr.

Kloveniers-

9

Groenburgwal

Zwanenburgwal

Waterloo-plein

Stadhuis

Muziek-theater

Rokin
Rokin

Nieuwe Doelenstr.

Staal-straat

Heiligeweg

Konings-plein

Singel

Munt-plein

Binnenamstel

Amstel

Blauwbrug

Herengracht

Reguliersdwarsstraat

Reguliersbree-straat

Rembrandt-plein

Amstelstraat

Amstel

1 Begijnhof
2 Spui
3' Café Luxembourg
4 Gebed Zonder End
5 Huis aan de Drie Grachten
6 Agnietenkapel
7' Atrium
8 Oudemanhuispoort

9 Poppenhuis
10 Trippenhuis
11 Oost-Indisch Huis (East India House)
12 Amsterdam's Narrowest House
13 De Waag
14 Ons' Lieve Heer op Solder
15 Red Light District

This walk takes you into the heart of the oldest part of the city, where you can see the oldest remaining structure in Amsterdam as well as the city's narrowest house. This is the core of Amsterdam, the epicenter from which the city expanded into other directions. Take this walk in the afternoon if you can, and leave yourself some time to people-watch at one of the city's notable cafes. The walk ends near the Red Light District. START: **Begijnhof (tram 1, 2, 4, 5, 9, 14, 16, 24, or 25 to Spui).**

1 ★★ Begijnhof. This cluster of small homes around a leafy garden courtyard is the best place to appreciate the history of old Amsterdam. No. 34 is the city's oldest house, built around 1455, and is one of only two timber houses remaining in the city. Amsterdam was a destination for religious pilgrims and an important Catholic center. The Begijnhof (a cloister) offered devout women the option to live without a husband and children, and without becoming a nun, at a time when there was little in the way of alternatives. It remained in operation even after the 1578 changeover of the city from Catholicism to Protestantism. The last *begijn* died in 1971, but you can still pay homage to these pious women by pausing for a moment at the small flower-planed mound that lies just at the center garden's edge, across from the Engelse Kerk (English Church), which dates to 1607. Opposite the front of the church, at no. 30, is the Begijnhofkapel, a secret Catholic chapel from 1671 that's still in use

Spui.

today. The houses are now a home for seniors. 🕐 *30 min. Spui & Gedempte Begijnensloot. No phone. Free admission. Daily 9am–5pm.*

2 Spui. This square is both elegant and animated. At its south end is a statue of a small boy, *Het Lieverdje (The Little Darling),* who is supposed to represent a typical Amsterdam child. Across the street, at no. 21, is the Maagdenhuis, the main downtown building of the University of Amsterdam. *Spui.*

The Begijnhof garden.

3 ★ **Café Luxembourg.** The *New York Times* named this bohemian place "one of the world's greatest cafes." The sidewalk tables are a wonderful place to people-watch in summer while enjoying a toasted Gouda sandwich and a cup of strong Dutch coffee (ideally not served with the typical syrupy-sweet condensed milk). *Spuistraat 24 (at Spui).* ☎ *020/620-6264.* *$$.*

4 **Gebed Zonder End.** This tiny alleyway is located in the district known as De Wallen (The Walls), and its name, which means "prayer without end," comes from the convents that used to be here. Legend has it that you could always hear the murmur of prayers from behind the walls. You are in the heart of Old Amsterdam here—the streets are narrow and a bit confusing. *To reach the alleyway, go to the end of Spui and cross Rokin and Nes, walking along Lange Brugsteeg to Grimburgwal.*

5 **Huis aan de Drie Grachten (House on the Three Canals).** Continue on Grimburgwal and cross Oudezijds Voorburgwal and Oudezijds Achterburgwal. Between these

The redbrick House on the Three Canals.

Oudemanhuispoort is home to a secondhand-book market.

two canals, you'll find this restored handsome redbrick, step-gabled, Dutch Renaissance house from 1609, with red-painted wooden shutters. *Oudezijds Voorburgwal 249.*

6 **Agnietenkapel.** Stroll a short way along Oudezijds Voorburgwal canal to no. 231, where you'll spot an elaborately ornamental gateway from 1571. This leads to the chapel (1470) of what was the St. Agnes Convent until the Protestant takeover of Amsterdam. It later formed part of the Athenaeum Illustre, the city's first university, and now houses a University of Amsterdam function suite. *Oudezijds Voorburgwal 231.*

7 **Atrium.** Students, professors, and regular humans in search of cheap, sustaining nosh congregate in the casual self-service mensa (student restaurant) at the University of Amsterdam. The menu mixes standard Dutch fare like salads and pea-and-ham soup with exotic influences like Indonesian bami (noodle) and nasi (rice) croquettes. None are produced to any memorable effect, but they're edible. *Oudezijds Achterburgwal 237 (at Grimburgwal).* ☎ 020/525-3999. \$.

Poppenhuis mansion.

❽ **Oudemanhuispoort.** Backtrack to the House on the Three Canals and cross the bridge to the far side of Oudezijds Achterburgwal. You'll pass the Gasthuis, once a hospital and now part of the University of Amsterdam campus, and turn right into a dimly lit arcade, the Oudemanhuispoort, that hosts a secondhand-book market Monday to Saturday 10am to 6pm. If you're interested, browse around here for a few minutes. In the middle of the arcade, on the left, you'll see a doorway leading to a courtyard garden with a statue of Minerva. It's a lovely place for a few quiet minutes of peace. *Off Grimburgwal.*

❾ **Poppenhuis.** Turn right on Kloveniersburgwal and cross over the canal and go left to reach this handsome classical mansion built in 1642 for Joan Poppen, a dissolute grandson and heir to a rich German merchant. *Kloveniersburgwal 95.*

❿ **Trippenhuis.** Nearby you'll see this house built between 1660 and 1664 for the Trip brothers, who were arms dealers (which explains the martial images and emblems dotted about the house). Originally there were two houses behind a single classical facade, but the two have

since been joined. It now houses the Royal Netherlands Academy of Arts and Sciences and is not open for visitors. *Kloveniersburgwal 29.*

⓫ **Oost-Indisch Huis (East India House).** Backtrack to the canal bridge and cross over to Oude Hoogstraat, where you can enter this impressive 1606 building via a courtyard on the left side of the street. Once the headquarters of the Vereenigde Oostindische Compagnie, or V.O.C. (United East India Company), the house now belongs to the University of Amsterdam. It's not officially open for visits, but you can stroll into the courtyard and through the doors to take a peek at the hallways hung with paintings of the 17th-century Dutch trading settlement of Batavia (now Jakarta, Indonesia). *Oude Hoogstraat 24.*

Oost-Indisch Huis (East India House).

Amsterdam's Narrowest House.

12 Amsterdam's Narrowest House. Next door, at Oude Hoogstraat 22, is the city's narrowest house, just 2m (6½ ft.) wide. Backtrack to Kloveniersburgwal and go left. At no. 26 you'll see another narrow house, the Klein Trippenhuis, the house of the Trip brothers' coachman (p 28, **3**). A few doors down, at nos. 10–12, is the drugstore Jacob Hooy & Co., which has been dispensing medicinal relief since 1743.

13 De Waag (Weigh House). Kloveniersburgwal ends at Nieuwmarkt, a large square where you'll easily spot the massive edifice that was once one of the city's medieval gates, and later the Weigh House and guild offices. Nieuwmarkt is the gateway to both the city's Chinatown and Red Light District. Small, family-run Chinese restaurants abound here. *Nieuwmarkt. See p 28,* **1**.

14 ★ Ons' Lieve Heer op Solder (Our Lord in the Attic). Stroll down Zeedijk and cross over the canal. After Amsterdam's 1578 Protestant *Alteratie* (Changeover), Roman Catholics fell into disfavor. Forced to worship in secret, they devised ingenious ways of gathering for Sunday services. This museum incorporates the most amazing of these clandestine places of worship. The church is in the attic of one of the oldest canal houses you can visit, which was transformed between 1661 and 1663 by wealthy Catholic merchant Jan Hartman to house a church. Worshipers entered by a door on a side street and climbed a narrow flight of stairs to the hidden third-floor church, with its large baroque altar and pews to seat 150. ⏱ *30 min. Oudezijds Voorburgwal 40.* ☎ *020/624-6604. www. opsolder.nl. Admission 8€ adults, 4€ students & kids 6–18. Mon–Sat 10am– 5pm, Sun & holidays 1–5pm. Closed Jan 1 & Apr 30. Metro: Nieuwmarkt.*

15 Red Light District. This is a good chance to tour the Red Light District (p 14, **8**). To do that, take Monnickenstraat to Oudezijds Achterburgwal and turn right, and you'll find many windows that frame prostitutes waiting for customers. When you're finished strolling, you can catch the Metro from Nieuwmarkt station or walk the 10 minutes to Centraal Station or the Dam to catch a tram. ●

Shopping at de Bijenkorf

After all this history, you may be eager to return to the modern age—and what better way than through some rampant consumerism? Amsterdam's best department store, de Bijenkorf (the Beehive; p 72) sells a terrific variety of goods. If you forgot something at home, you can probably find a replacement here.

Shopping **Best Bets**

Best **Wine Store**
★ Wijnhandel De Ware Jacob, *Herenstraat 41 (p 76)*

Best **Antiques**
★ Premsela & Hamburger, *Pieter Cornelisz Hooftstraat (p 70)*

Best **Delftware**
★★ Jorrit Heinen, *Prinsengracht 440 (p 72)*

Best **English-Language Bookstore**
★ American Book Center, *Spui 12 (p 70)*

Best **Place to Score Castro's Favorite Stogies**
★ P.G.C. Hajenius, *Rokin 92–96 (p 71)*

Best **Place to Shop for Diamonds**
★ Gassan Diamonds, *Nieuwe Uilenburgerstraat 173–175 (p 74)*

Best **Place to Pick Up Authentic Hunks of Gouda**
★ De Kaaskamer van Amsterdam, *Runstraat 7 (p 71)*

Best **Dutch Designer Shoes**
★★ Jan Jansen, *Roelof Hartstraat 16 (p 76)*

Best **Street Market**
★★ Albert Cuypmarkt, *Albert Cuypstraat (p 75)*

Best **Place to Provision for Romance**
E. Kramer-Pontifex, *Reestraat 18–20 (p 71)*

Best **Place to Stop and Smell the Flowers**
★ Bloemenmarkt (Flower Market), *along the south bank of Singel btw. Muntplein and Koningsplein (p 75)*

Best **Place to Shop for Picnic Provisions**
★ Boerenmarkt (Farmers Market), *Noordermarkt (p 75)*

Best **Place to Shop for Gifts for Friends Back Home**
Lush, *Kalverstraat 98 (p 76)*

Best **Department Store**
★★ Metz&Co, *Leidsestraat 34–36 (p 72)*

Best **Designer Boutique for Men, Women & Teens**
★ Azzurro Due, *Pieter Cornelisz Hooftstraat 138 (p 73)*

Best **Unusual Kids' Toys**
Tinkerbell, *Spiegelgracht 10–12 (p 75)*

Best **Designer Goods at Discount Prices**
★ Megazino, *Rozengracht 207–213 (p 73)*

Best **Artisan Chocolates**
★ Puccini Bomboni, *Staalstraat 17 (p 71).*

Previous page: Magna Plaza's elegant interior. This page: An antique silver spoon set and platter.

Museum District **Shopping**

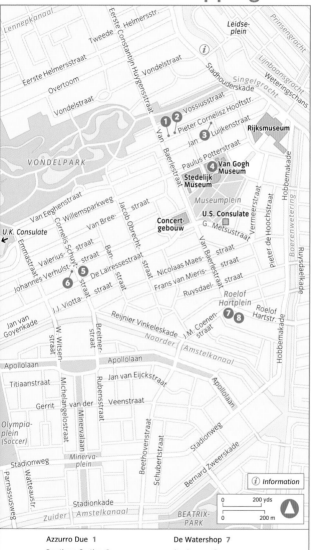

Azzurro Due 1	De Watershop 7
Boutique Cartier 2	Jan Jansen 8
Charly Amsterdam 5	Louis Vuitton 3
Charly Ensuite 6	Van Gogh Museum Shop 4

Central Amsterdam **Shopping**

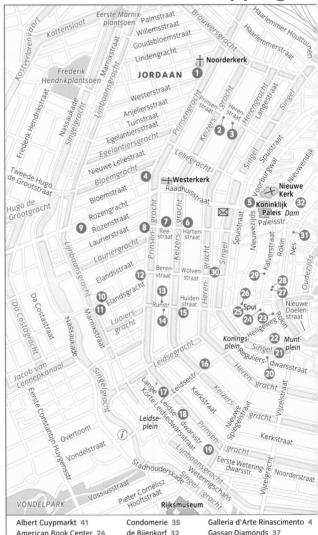

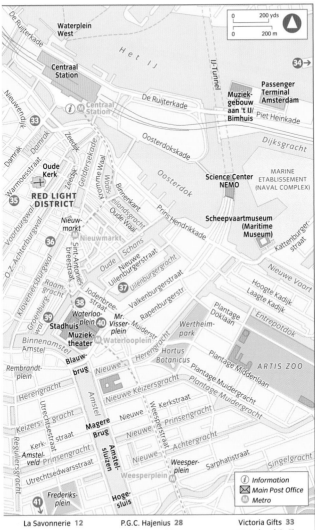

Amsterdam Shopping A to Z

If you can't afford the real thing, shop for prints, reproductions, and more at the Van Gogh Museum Shop.

Art & Antiques

Mathieu Hart OLD CENTER Since 1878, this refined store has been selling color etchings of Dutch cities, rare old prints, 18th-century delftware, and grandfather clocks. *Rokin 122 (at Spui).* ☎ *020/623-1658. www.hart antiques.com. AE, MC, V. Tram: 4, 9, 14, 16, 24, or 25 to Spui. Map p 68.*

★★ Premsela & Hamburger OLD CENTER Opened in 1823, this fine jewelry and antique silver seller boasts a great collection of Old Dutch silver by 17th-century craftsmen. *Rokin 98 (at Spui).* ☎ *020/624-9688. www. premsela.com. AE, MC, V. Tram: 4, 9, 14, 16, 24, or 25 to Spui. Map p 68.*

Peruse thousands of books at the American Book Center.

Van Gogh Museum Shop

MUSEUM DISTRICT This starry store sells everything from imitations of van Gogh classics to mugs painted with his famous sunflowers, plus art books. *Paulus Potterstraat 7 (at Museumplein).* ☎ *020/570-5200. www.vangoghmuseum.nl. AE, DC, MC, V. Tram: 2, 3, 5, or 12 to Van Baerlestraat; 16 or 24 to Museumplein. Map p 67.*

Books

★ American Book Center OLD CENTER From novels and Frommer's guides to the latest magazines, this large U.S.-style bookstore is extremely well stocked. *Spui 12 (at Spuistraat).* ☎ *020/625-5537. www.abc.nl. AE, MC, V. Tram: 1, 2, or 5 to Spui. Map p 68.*

Evenaar CANAL BELT Specializing in travel literature, this store has everything from travel guides and world maps to books on armchair travel and anthropology, and antique travel books. *Singel 348 (at Wolvenstraat).* ☎ *020/624-6289. www.evenaar.net. AE, MC, V. Tram: 1, 2, or 5 to Spui. Map p 68.*

Waterstone's OLD CENTER This British chain is well stocked with the latest fiction and nonfiction releases.

You may have a hard time choosing from the hundreds of cheeses for sale at De Kaas-kamer van Amsterdam.

You'll find lots of hardcovers here, but they have a wide selection of paperbacks as well. *Kalverstraat 152 (at Spui).* ☎ *020/638-3821. www. waterstones.com. AE, DC, MC, V. Tram: 1, 2, 4, 5, 14, 16, 24, or 25 to Spui. Map p 68.*

Candles

E. Kramer-Pontifex CANAL BELT All kinds of candles are sold here, from elaborately carved melting works of art to kitsch designs. Pick up scented candles and votives for a romantic evening in your hotel room. *Reestraat 18–20 (at Prinsengracht).* ☎ *020/626-5274. http:// sites.google.com/site/pontifexkramer/ home. MC, V. Tram: 13, 14, or 17 to Westermarkt. Map p 68.*

Cheese

★ **De Kaaskamer van Amsterdam** CANAL BELT   Choose from more than 300 cheeses (they will vacuum-pack for travelers), including rows and rows of Gouda wheels stamped with their farm of origin. *Runstraat 7 (at Keizersgracht).* ☎ *020/ 623-3483. www.kaaskamer.nl. MC, V. Tram: 1, 2, or 5 to Spui. Map p 68.*

Chocolates

★ **Puccini Bomboni** OLD CENTER A long, open table supports fresh handmade pralines in a plethora of shapes and styles—pure, milk, and white; liqueur-filled and alcohol-free varieties. *Staalstraat 17 (at Waterlooplein).* ☎ *020/626-5474. www.puccinibomboni.com. MC, V.*

Tram: 9 or 14 to Waterlooplein. Map p 68.

Cigars & Pipes

★ **P.G.C. Hajenius** OLD CENTER In business since 1826, this store is the best place to shop for Cuban cigars—there's an entire room stocked with Havanas. You'll also find Dutch handmade clay pipes. *Rokin 92–96 (at Spui).* ☎ *020/623-7494. www.hajenius.com. AE, DC, MC, V. Tram: 4, 9, 14, 16, 24, or 25 to Spui. Map p 68.*

Smokiana CANAL BELT   In addition to pipe tobacco, this specialist pipe store sells just about every kind of pipe imaginable, from the antique to the exotic to the kitsch to the downright weird. In addition, the store hosts a pipe museum. *Prinsengracht 488 (at Leidsestraat).* ☎ *020/ 421-1779. www.pipeshop.nl. MC, V. Tram: 1, 2, or 5 to Prinsengracht. Map p 68.*

Cigar lovers can pick up some fine Cubans in Amsterdam.

Hand-painted delftware makes a great gift.

Delftware

Galleria d'Arte Rinascimento
CANAL BELT   This emporium sells porcelain of every type, from quality-challenged "delftware" to genuine hand-painted delftware from De Koninklijke Porceleyne Fles (Royal Delft), along with multicolored, and pricey, Makkumware from Koninklijke Tichelaar Makkum. *Prinsengracht 170 (at Bloemstraat).* ☎ *020/622-7509. www.delft-art-gallery.com. AE, DC, MC, V. Tram: 13, 14, or 17 to Westermarkt. Map p 68.*

★★ **Jorrit Heinen** CANAL BELT
One of a family-owned chain that makes and sells their own-brand porcelain. They are also official dealers of delftware, Makkumware, fine crystal, and other quality gifts. *Prinsengracht 440 (at Leidsestraat).* ☎ *020/627-8299. www.jorritheinen. com. AE, MC, V. Tram: 1, 2, or 5 to Prinsengracht. Map p 68.*

Department Stores

★ **de Bijenkorf** OLD CENTER   The city's best-known department store sports the largest variety of goods. From handbags to big-screen TVs, it's all here. *Dam 1.*

Amsterdam is a great place to shop for contemporary home furnishings, like this chair.

☎ *0900/0919. www.bijenkorf.nl. AE, MC, V. Tram: 4, 9, 14, 16, 24, or 25 to the Dam. Map p 68.*

HEMA OLD CENTER   This smaller store is a great place to find a cheap item (gloves, hat, socks) or just a toothbrush. *Kalvertoren, Kalverstraat 212 (at Muntplein).* ☎ *020/422-8988. www.hema.nl. No credit cards. Tram: 4, 9, 14, 16, 24, or 25 to Muntplein. Map p 68.*

★★ **Metz&Co** CANAL BELT
Founded in 1740, this is Amsterdam's most upscale department store, selling everything from beautiful furniture to gourmet kitchenware. Check out the rooftop (sixth-floor) cafe/restaurant **M'Café**, with its fantastic city views. *Leidsestraat 34–36 (at Keizersgracht).* ☎ *020/520-7020. www.metzco.eu. AE, DC, MC, V. Tram: 1, 2, or 5 to Keizersgracht. Map p 68.*

Design & Home Furnishings

★ **Pol's Potten**
KNSM-EILAND
This interior-design store in the redeveloping Eastern Harbor area is a good place for furnishings, accessories, kitchenware, and household knickknacks

by hip young designers. *KNSM-Laan 39 (at Azartplein).* ☎ *020/419-3541. www.polspotten.nl. MC, V. Tram: 10 to Azartplein.*

Fashion

★ **Analik** CANAL BELT Owned by one of Amsterdam's renowned designers, Analik, this store has one room filled with small pieces of clothing for young and skinny women, and another with funky handbags and other accessories designed by Dutch artists. *Hartenstraat 36 (at Keizersgracht).* ☎ *020/ 422-0561. www.analik.com. AE, MC, V. Tram: 13, 14, or 17 to Westermarkt. Map p 68.*

★ **Azzurro Due** MUSEUM DISTRICT The ultimate address for finding a pair of designer jeans or that elusive Prada accessory for both men and women. Very chic, very trendy. *Pieter Cornelisz Hooftstraat 138.* ☎ *020/671-9708. www.azzurrofashiongroup.nl. AE, DC, MC, V. Tram: 2, 3, 5, or 12 to Van Baerlestraat. Map p 67.*

★ **Charly Ensuite & Charly Amsterdam** MUSEUM DISTRICT Charly Ensuite specializes in catwalk fashions from the likes of Alexander McQueen, Diane von Fürstenberg, Giambattista Valli, Dusan, and Yigal Azrouël. Cross the street to Charly Amsterdam for casual apparel and accessories by Rosemunde, Barong Barong, Fabrizio Giannone, MVN, Tritoni, and more. *Charly Ensuite: Cornelis Schuytstraat 48 (at Johannes Verhulststraat).* ☎ *020/670-1370. www.charlyensuite.nl. Charly Amsterdam: Cornelis Schuytstraat 45.* ☎ *020/672-0404. AE, MC, V. Tram: 2 to Cornelis Schuytstraat. Map p 67.*

Louis Vuitton MUSEUM DISTRICT Of course, you'll find the usual upmarket suitcases and handbags here that Vuitton is famous for, but also a good selection of shoes, jewelry, belts, and ties. *Pieter Cornelisz*

Shoppers can find all sorts of designer goods in Amsterdam, like these purses from Azzurro Due.

Hooftstraat 65–67 (at Honthorststraat). ☎ *020/575-5775. www.louisvuitton. com. AE, DC, MC, V. Tram: 2, 3, 5, or 12 to Van Baerlestraat. Map p 67.*

★ **Megazino** JORDAAN Large for Amsterdam, this designer outlet sells everything from Armani, Gucci, and Prada to Calvin Klein and Dolce & Gabbana—all at 30% to 50% off the original price. *Rozengracht 207–213 (at Lijnbaansgracht).* ☎ *020/330-1031. www.megazino.com. AE, MC, V. Tram: 13, 14, or 17 to Westermarkt. Map p 68.*

★★ **Van Ravenstein** CANAL BELT The latest creations by Dutch and Belgian designers and fashion houses such as Viktor & Rolf, Maison Martin Margiela, Dries Van Noten, Anne Demeulemeester, and more, are this small boutique's stock-in-trade. *Keizersgracht 359 (at Huidenstraat).* ☎ *020/639-0067. www.van-ravenstein.nl. AE, MC, V. Tram: 1, 2, or 5 to Keizersgracht. Map p 68.*

★ **Webers Holland** OLD CENTER The venerable 17th-century Klein Trippenhuis (p 28) is the counterintuitive setting for this avant-garde, sexy, humorous—and, to a degree, in-your-face—store for women. *Kloveniersburgwal 26 (at Nieuwmarkt).* ☎ *020/638-1777. www.webers holland.nl. MC, V. Metro: Nieuwmarkt. Map p 68.*

Flowers

Bloomings-Amsterdam CANAL BELT   Orchids and other exotic plants, oriental lilies, special tropical flowers, and all kinds of tasteful accessories give this Jordaan store a delicate look to go along with the scents. *Elandsgracht 134 (at Lijnbaansgracht).* ☎ *06/2421-3723. www.bloomings-amsterdam.nl. MC, V. Tram: 7, 10, or 17 to Elandsgracht. Map p 68.*

★ **Gerda's Bloemen** CANAL BELT   This elegant florist boasts a fantastic selection of exotic flowers and unusual plants artfully arranged and presented. *Runstraat 16 (at Keizersgracht).* ☎ *020/624-2912. MC, V. Tram: 1, 2, or 5 to Spui. Map p 68.*

Funky Stores

Condomerie OLD CENTER   Handily sited on the edge of the Red Light District, this condom boutique stocks a vast range of these singular items, in all shapes, sizes, and flavors, from common brands to flashy designer fittings. *Warmoesstraat 141 (behind de Bijenkorf).* ☎ *020/627-4174. www.condomerie.com. AE, MC, V. Tram: 4, 9, 14, 16, 24, or 25 to the Dam. Map p 68.*

Episode WATERLOOPLEIN   Jackets, dresses, scarves, belts, funky brooches, boots—you'll find all these

Amsterdam's florists sell fresh bouquets and flower arrangements.

and more at this unisex vintage store. Specialties include flamboyant evening gowns and leather jackets, all in pretty good shape and reasonably priced. *Waterlooplein 1.* ☎ *020/320-3000. www.episode.eu. MC, V. Tram: 9 or 14 to Waterlooplein. Map p 68.*

kids 't Curiosa Winkeltje CANAL BELT   This funky but fun store sells modern versions of old tin cars, colored bottles and glasses, lamps shaped like bananas, and children's toys from the 1950s. *Prinsengracht 228 (at Laurierstraat).* ☎ *020/625-1352. MC, V. Tram: 13, 14, or 17 to Westermarkt. Map p 68.*

The Magic Mushroom Gallery CANAL BELT   For everything from "psychoactive mushrooms" to tonics such as Yohimbe Rush and Horn E that allegedly improve your sex life. *Singel 524 (at the Flower Market).* ☎ *020/422-7845. www.magicmushroom.com. MC, V. Tram: 4, 9, 14, 16, 24, or 25 to Muntplein. Map p 68.*

Jewelry

★ **Boutique Cartier** MUSEUM DISTRICT   You'll find intricately designed jewelry, watches, pens, and other accessories at this quintessential French store. *Pieter Cornelisz Hooftstraat 132–134 (at Van Baerlestraat).* ☎ *020/670-3434. www.cartier.com. AE, DC, MC, V. Tram: 2, 3, 5, or 12 to Van Baerlestraat. Map p 67.*

★ **Gassan Diamonds** OLD CENTER   In addition to shopping for diamonds, you can take a tour in the stunning Amsterdam School–style building that shows you how the jewels are cut. *Nieuwe Uilenburgerstraat 173–175 (off Jodenbreestraat).* ☎ *020/622-5333. www.gassandiamonds.nl. AE, DC, MC, V. Tram: 9 or 14 to Waterlooplein. Map p 68.*

★ **Gort** CANAL BELT   This beautiful little store specializes in unique and innovative jewelry. If you like modern and minimalist designs, then this place is for you. *Herenstraat 11 (at Herengracht).* ☎ *020/620-6240. www.juweliergort.nl. MC, V. Tram: 13, 14, or 17 to Westermarkt. Map p 68.*

Kids
kids Tinkerbell CANAL BELT This unique store sells modern versions of old wood toys. A great place to find an unusual gift for a child. *Spiegelgracht 10–12 (at Prinsengracht).* ☎ *020/625-8830. www.tinkerbell toys.nl. MC, V. Tram: 7 or 10 to Spiegelgracht. Map p 68.*

Malls
★★ Magna Plaza OLD CENTER Housed in the city's former main post office, from 1899, the elegant mall has four floors and 40 specialist stores, from the Björn Borg Store to Swarovski. *Nieuwezijds Voorburgwal 182 (at the Dam).* ☎ *020/570-3570. www.magnaplaza.nl. Credit cards accepted in most stores. Tram: 1, 2, 5, 13, 14, or 17 to the Dam. Map p 68.*

Markets
★★ Albert Cuypmarkt DE PIJP Amsterdam's most-frequented all-purpose street market stretches for 1km (½ mile). From fresh herring and Gouda to silk scarves and hand-knitted hats, you'll find it here Monday to Saturday 9am to 6pm. *Albert Cuypstraat (btw. Ferdinand Bolstraat & Van Woustraat). No phone. www.albertcuypmarkt.com. No credit cards. Tram: 16 or 24 to Albert Cuypstraat. Map p 68.*

Artplein Spui OLD CENTER Every Sunday (9am–5pm) from March to December, local artists mount outdoor exhibits here. You may have to wade through some mediocrity, but it's possible to find something special. *Spui.* ☎ *0343/516476. www.artpleinspui.nl. No credit cards. Tram: 1, 2, or 5 to Spui. Map p 68.*

★ Bloemenmarkt (Flower Market) CANAL BELT Partly floating on a row of permanently moored

Gassan Diamonds offers an informative tour in addition to dazzling jewelry.

barges, this is Amsterdam's most popular flower market. You'll find fresh-cut flowers, bright plants, rows and rows of tulip bunches, and ready-to-travel packets of tulip bulbs. Open daily 9am to 6pm. *Along the south bank of Singel btw. Muntplein & Koningsplein. No phone. No credit cards. Tram: 9, 14, 16, 24, or 25 to Muntplein; 1, 2, or 5 to Koningsplein. Map p 68.*

★ Boerenmarkt (Farmers Market) JORDAAN Also known as the Bio (or organic) market, it caters to trendy Jordaan locals. It's a great place to find fresh vegetables, fruit, cheeses, and organic breads for a picnic. Open Saturday 9am to 4pm. *Noordermarkt (at Prinsengracht). No phone. www.boerenmarktamsterdam.nl. No credit cards. Tram: 1, 2, 5, 13, or 17 to Martelaarsgracht. Map p 68.*

A vendor sells poffertjes, a small fluffy pancake, at the Albert Cuypmarkt.

Strolling in **Vondelpark**

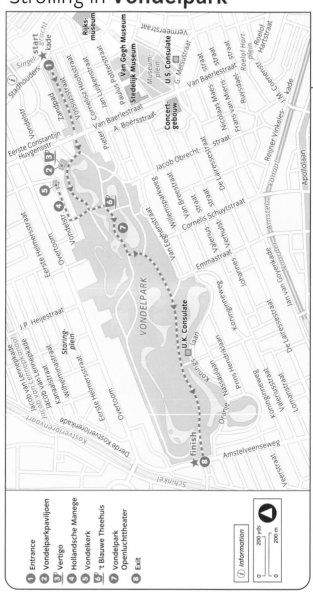

1 Entrance
2 Vondelparkpaviljoen
3 Vertigo
4 Hollandsche Manege
5 Vondelkerk
6 't Blauwe Theehuis
7 Vondelpark Openluchttheater
8 Exit

Information

0 — 200 yds
0 — 200 m

Previous page: Relaxing in green Vondelpark.

A Rollerblading Tour, Anyone?

If you're game for a little rollerblading, try joining the hundreds of skaters (they once had a record 3,000) who strap on their 'blades for Amsterdam's regular **Friday Night Skate** (www.fridaynight skate.com). This event begins at 8:30pm—meet up at 8pm in summer and 8:15pm in winter—from outside the Vondelpark Pavilion (formerly the Filmmuseum) in Vondelpark, and takes one of a series of possible routes of around 20km (12½ miles) through the city, returning to the starting point.

If you're up for it, join the hundreds of skaters who skate around the city for Friday Night Skate.

church designed by Petrus Josephus Hubertus Cuypers (architect of Centraal Station). It was completed in 1880. A fire in 1904 destroyed its original tower, and a new one was added by the architect's son. In 1985, the church was converted into offices, and cultural events are sometimes held here. *Vondelstraat 120.* ☎ *020/689-7920. Free admission. 1st Wed & 3rd Sun of month noon–4pm.*

6 't Blauwe Theehuis. The "Blue Teahouse" is a functionalist-style circular cafe from 1937 on two levels, with a park-level open-air terrace and an upstairs balcony terrace. It's a fine place for indulging in a coffee and croissant. At night, there's dancing and live music. *Vondelpark 5.* ☎ *020/662-0254. $.*

7 ★ kids **Vondelpark Openluchttheater (Vondelpark Open-Air Theater).** Another few minutes' stroll brings you to this open-air venue where summer musical concerts, occasional theater pieces (usually in Dutch), and children's shows (usually in Dutch, but emphasis is on mime and sometimes puppets, so children of all nationalities seem to enjoy the show) are staged free of charge. Performances take place June through the third week of August at various times. ☎ *020/428-3360. www.openluchttheater.nl. Free admission.*

8 Exit. By the time you reach the western gates, you'll have walked a little over 2km (1¼ miles). You can exit here and jump on tram 1 from Overtoom (from the Overtoomsesluis stop) or 2 from Koninginneweg (from the Valeriusplein stop) to Centraal Station, or you can head back east, staying to your right to take the path back to the entrance gates close to Leidseplein. The entire loop measures about 4km (2½ miles).

Touring Amsterdam by **Canal Bike**

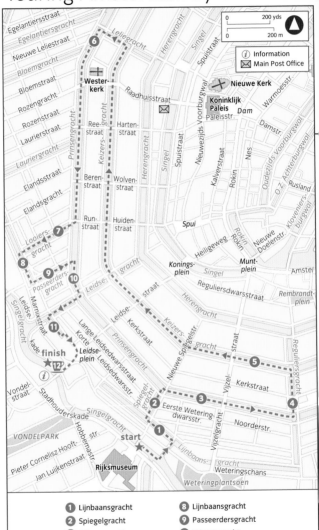

1. Lijnbaansgracht
2. Spiegelgracht
3. Prinsengracht
4. Reguliersgracht
5. Keizersgracht
6. Prinsengracht
7. Looiersgracht
8. Lijnbaansgracht
9. Passeerdersgracht
10. Prinsengracht and Leidsegracht
11. Leidsebosje
12. Café Americain

Canal biking down the city's myriad waterways is an outdoor activity unique to Amsterdam. These pedal boats (or pedalos) let you glide quietly down the canals for a close-up look at houseboats and bridges. You'll also get to admire the many 17th- and 18th-century houses that line the canals from a different vantage point. I don't recommend taking very young kids on the "bikes," but older children will likely remember the experience for the rest of their lives. Early on a summer's evening or late on a winter's afternoon is the best time, when the slanting sun hits the buildings and bridges, affording rich opportunities for photos. START: **Tram 7 or 10 to Spiegelgracht for the Rijksmuseum mooring on the Singelgracht canal.**

1 Lijnbaansgracht. From the Rijksmuseum mooring, take a left on Lijnbaansgracht canal, with its very low bridge and rows of neck-gabled houses. It's a very long canal that provided rope makers (the name translates to "ropewalk") in the 17th century enough space to stretch and twist the ropes they made for the shipbuilding industry in Amsterdam.

2 ★ Spiegelgracht. Turn right onto this short canal lined with antiques shops. There are more than 70 specialized antiques dealers in this neighborhood, selling everything from barometers and clocks to brass and copper ornaments. If you choose to stop and have a look, be sure to leave one person in your

Lijnbaansgracht canal.

You can get a close-up view of houseboats and canal houses from the seat of a canal bike.

party with the canal bike—don't leave it unattended.

3 ★★★ Prinsengracht. Turn right onto one of Amsterdam's Golden Age canals. Many of the houses here were built around 1700. Several of them still have their original neck gables.

4 ★ Reguliersgracht. Turn left onto Reguliersgracht. You can spot seven identical arched bridges, perfectly aligned, spanning this canal. These date back to the 17th century. It's a pretty spot for photographs.

5 ★★★ Keizersgracht. Turn left onto Keizersgracht, the city's widest canal at 28m (92 ft.). Some of the houses lining the canal were built as

Reguliersgracht canal has seven identical arched bridges that are perfectly aligned.

coach houses for the mansions of the prosperous "Golden Bend" stretch of nearby Herengracht. You'll be pedaling for quite some time (30–45 min.) on Keizersgracht as it winds through the edge of the old center and up toward Centraal Station and into the Jordaan. To begin looping back, turn left on tiny Leliegracht, and then left again on Prinsengracht.

6 ★★★ **Prinsengracht.** You are back on Prinsengracht, but now you are in the heart of the elegant and charming Jordaan neighborhood. The Anne Frank House is here, and the tall spire of the Westerkerk, the largest reformed church in Holland, will be visible to your right. You'll

You can spot the tall spire of the Westerkerk from Prinsengracht Canal.

see many houseboats lining the banks of Prinsengracht; most of them have been here since just after World War II, when the housing shortage forced some people to find alternative dwellings. There are currently some 2,400 houseboats in Amsterdam, and no further permits will be issued for new ones.

7 **Looiersgracht.** Turn right at the "Tanners' Canal"; not surprisingly, this is where leather used to be tanned.

8 **Lijnbaansgracht.** Turn left on the long canal that you pedaled on earlier.

9 ★★★ **Passeerdersgracht.** Turn left here and notice the low railing on the bridge that stops cars from falling into the water. Before the railing was built, cars frequently fell into the canal, and in the 18th century, horses and carriages also tumbled into the water. The railings were not installed until the 1960s—on all 100km (62 miles) of Amsterdam's canals.

10 **Prinsengracht and Leidsegracht.** Turn right and you're on Prinsengracht again. Turn right onto Leidsegracht. Notice the four houses at nos. 72–78, which display four different kinds of gables: No. 72 has a neck gable, 74 a cornice gable, 76 a spout gable, and 78 a step gable (see the box "Gables 101" on p 51 for a primer on gables).

Canal Bike Rentals & Rules

Canal bikes have seats for up to four people (a child can be carried as a fifth passenger in some circumstances). They are stable and comfortable. The charge per head for one or two people is 8€ for 1 hour, 11€ for 1½ hours, and 14€ for 2 hours; and for more than two people 7€, 10€, and 13€, respectively. The above itinerary will take about 2 hours, a bit longer if you go slowly. You'll need a credit card, a 50€ refundable deposit (which can go on the card), and an ID to rent your canal bike. Rental hours are 10am to between 6 and 9:30pm (depending on the weather) June to September; and 10am to 5:30pm the rest of the year (in winter, only when the weather is tolerable). Rent from **Canal Bike,** at the Rijksmuseum mooring on Singelgracht (☎ 0900/333-4442; www.canal.nl). In addition to this mooring, there are docks in front of the Anne Frank House, Leideplein (facing the American Hotel), and at the corner of Keizersgracht and Leidsestraat (closed in winter). If you get tired, you can always drop off your canal bike at one of these moorings and receive your refundable deposit back.

Always stay to the right in the canals—this is especially important when going under bridges in narrow canals. All other traffic has right of way. The port area and the Amstel River are off-limits to canal bikes. If you need a break, stop at one of the mooring docks. **Never** leave your canal bike unattended—it will be towed away.

⑪ Leidsebosje. Turn left and you'll spot the large Art Nouveau American Hotel opposite the mooring. You've reached the end! Return your canal bike here.

⑫ ★★ Café Americain. Overlooking Leidseplein, this turn-of-the-20th-century cafe is a national monument of Dutch Art Nouveau. The infamous spy Mata Hari had her wedding reception here. Don't forget to look up to admire the frosted-glass Tiffany chandeliers. There are plenty of salads, soups, and sandwiches to choose from. *In the Eden Amsterdam American Hotel, Leidsekade 97 (at Leidseplein).* ☎ *020/556-3000.* $$.

You'll spot many tour boats from the seat of your canal bike.

Biking Along the **Amstel River**

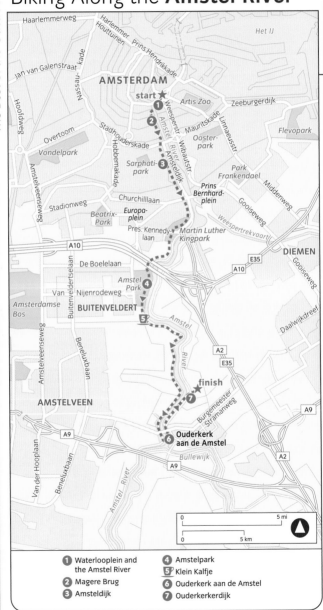

1. Waterlooplein and the Amstel River
2. Magere Brug
3. Amsteldijk
4. Amstelpark
5. Klein Kalfje
6. Ouderkerk aan de Amstel
7. Ouderkerkerdijk

Amsterdammers go everywhere on their bikes and don't particularly enjoy it when inexperienced visitors on a rented *fiets* (as a bicycle is called here) attempt to navigate the inner city's complicated streets and alleyways. This bike route takes you away from the city center and out to more pleasant and tranquil surroundings. START: **Tram 9 or 14 to Waterlooplein.**

Traveling the city by bike is a way of life for many Amsterdammers.

1 Waterlooplein and the Amstel River. Once you've rented your bikes (see the box "Renting Your Bikes," below), head south along the Amstel on Amsteldijk. Keep your eye out for houseboats moored along both banks and for a lot of other boat activity on the river. The Amstel will be to your left; on the return, you'll be on the far bank, with the river once again on your left.

2 ★ Magere Brug (Skinny Bridge). The Skinny Bridge over the Amstel is actually an 18th-century replacement of the original 17th-century bridge. It's a double drawbridge made of African azobé wood. Hundreds of lights illuminate the bridge at night. The Theater Carré, one of the city's largest theaters, is visible from the bridge.

3 Amsteldijk. As you pedal south, you'll need to cross busy Stadhouderskade. Continue on Amsteldijk south to the Berlagebrug (Berlage Bridge), where the traffic thickens again. Stay on Amsteldijk—most of the road traffic swings away to the right on President Kennedylaan. The road becomes noticeably quieter, almost rural, and you can relax and admire the many houseboats lined along the banks of the river.

Biking across the Skinny Bridge is a unique experience.

Enjoy peaceful views of the canals, rivers, and parks as you pedal through the city.

4 Amstelpark. Go under the highway bridge (A10 ring road) and continue along the riverbank until you reach this often quiet park. There's a statue of Rembrandt and a windmill at the end of the park, so continue pedaling to the south until you see them. It's a classic Dutch scene and perfect for a little rest and a photo or two. At this point, you'll probably want to stretch your legs and have a snack.

5 Klein Kalfje. This Dutch cafe-restaurant has a great sheltered terrace along the water (separated from the restaurant by the riverside road). Try the Dutch pea soup or a filling salad. Consider fueling up for your ride back with a strong Dutch coffee. *Amsteldijk-Noord 355 (at Kalfjeslaan).* ☎ *020/644-5338. $$.*

6 ★ Ouderkerk aan de Amstel. Continue south, past villas and cottages, to this charming little village. If you have time, lock up your bikes by the river and meander through the village streets before heading back.

7 Ouderkerkerdijk. Head back north on the opposite bank. You'll find this a quieter and narrower road than the Amsteldijk, with much less traffic. When you reach the Berlagebrug again, you'll know you're getting close to your starting point. The streets are busier here, but stay on the right bank and enjoy the different vistas until you reach Waterlooplein. ●

Renting Your Bikes

The rental outlet closest to your starting point is MacBike at Waterlooplein 199 (☎ 020/620-0985; www.macbike.nl). To get there, take tram 9 or 14 to Waterlooplein. You'll need a passport and a 50€ deposit (cash or credit card; the deposit is refundable upon return of the bike). Rates (with insurance) begin at 8.50€ for 3 hours and 13€ for 1 day, for a bike that you brake by pedaling backward; and 12€ and 17€, respectively, for a bike with a normal handbrake. MacBike is open daily 9am to 5:45pm. The 1-day rental requires you to return the bike by closing time. A range of bikes is available, including tandems and six-speed touring bikes. There are two other MacBike rental outlets (same phone and web details): at Stationsplein 5 outside Centraal Station, and Weteringschans 2 at Leidseplein.

Dining Best Bets

Best Canal View
De Belhamel $$ *Brouwersgracht 60* (p 95)

Best When Money Is No Object
★★★ La Rive $$$$ *Professor Tulpplein 1 (p 97)*

Best Dutch Oysters from Zeeland
★ Le Pêcheur $$$ *Reguliersdwarsstraat 32 (p 97)*

Best Place for Dining with Your Shoes Off
★ Supperclub $$$ *Jonge Roelensteeg 21 (p 99)*

Best Young Celebrity Chef Hot Spot
★★ Fifteen Amsterdam $$ *Pakhuis Amsterdam, Jollemanhof 9 (p 96)*

Best Innovative Five-Course Menu
★★ Bordewijk $$$ *Noordermarkt 7 (p 94)*

Best Drop-Dead Gorgeous Decor
★★ Vinkeles $$$$ *Keizersgracht 384 (p 100)*

Best Upmarket Moroccan Cuisine
★ Mamouche $$ *Quellijnstraat 104 (p 98)*

Best for Trendy Parents with No Babysitter
★★ Wilhelmina-Dok $$ *Nordwal 1 (p 100)*

Best Traditional Dutch Pea Soup
Brasserie de Poort $$ *Nieuwezijds Voorburgwal 176–180 (p 94)*

Best Vegetarian
Golden Temple $ *Utrechtsestraat 126 (p 96)*

Best Neighborhood Seafood Place
★★ Albatros Seafoodhouse $$ *Westerstraat 264 (p 94)*

Best Fashionistas
Caffepc $$ *Pieter Cornelisz Hooftstraat 87 (p 95)*

Best for Dining Alfresco
★★ De Kas $$$ *Kamerlingh Onneslaan 3 (p 95)*

Best for Kids
The Pancake Bakery $ *Prinsengracht 191 (p 99)*

Best Late-Night Chinese
Nam Kee $ *Zeedijk 111–113 (p 98)*

Best Elegant Indonesian
★ Sama Sebo $$ *Pieter Cornelisz Hooftstraat 27 (p 98)*

Best for Pre-Concertgebouw Dining
Brasserie Keyzer $$ *Van Baerlestraat 96 (p 94)*

Previous page: Dine canalside at De Belhamel. This page: Dine like an Amsterdammer on raw herring and onions.

Museum District **Dining**

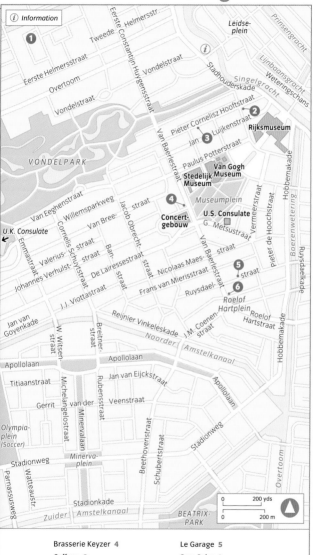

(i) Information

Eerste Helmersstr.

Tweede Helmersstr.

Leidse-plein

Prinsengracht

Lijnbaansgracht

Weteringschans

Singelgracht

Stadhouderskade

Eerste Helmersstraat

Overtoom

Vondelstraat

Eerste Constantijn Huygenstraat

Vondelstraat

Vondelstraat

(i)

Pieter Cornelisz Hooftstraat

Jan Luijkenstraat

Rijksmuseum

Van Baerlestraat

Paulus Potterstraat

VONDELPARK

Van Gogh Museum

Stedelijk Museum

Hobbemakade

Museumplein

Van Eeghenstraat

Willemsparkweg

Jacob... straat

Concert-gebouw

U.S. Consulate

G. Metsustraat

Vermeerstraat

Pieter de Hoochstraat

Boerenwetering

Ruysdaelkade

Van Bree-straat

Jacob Obrecht-straat

Cornelis Schuytstraat

U.K. Consulate

Emmastraat

Valerius-straat

De Lairessestraat

Ban-straat

Nicolaas Maes-straat

Van Baerlestraat

straat

Johannes Verhulst-straat

Frans van Mierisstraat

Ruysdael-straat

J.J. Viottastraat

Roelof Hartplein

Roelof Hartstraat

Jan van Goyenkade

W. Witsen-straat

Breitner-straat

Reijnier Vinkeleskade

J.M. Coenen-straat

Hobbemakade

Noorder Amstelkanaal

Apollolaan

Apollolaan

Jan van Eijckstraat

Apollolaan

Titiaanstraat

Michelangelostraat

Rubensstraat

Veenstraat

Gerrit van der

Minervalaan

Beethovenstraat

Stadionweg

Olympia-plein (Soccer)

Schubertstraat

Stadionweg

Parnassusweg

Watteaustr.

Minerva-plein

Zuider Amstelkanaal

Stadionkade

BEATRIX-PARK

Overtoom

| 0 | 200 yds |
| 0 | 200 m |

Central Amsterdam **Dining**

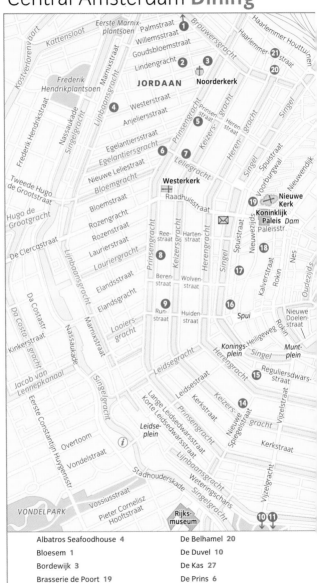

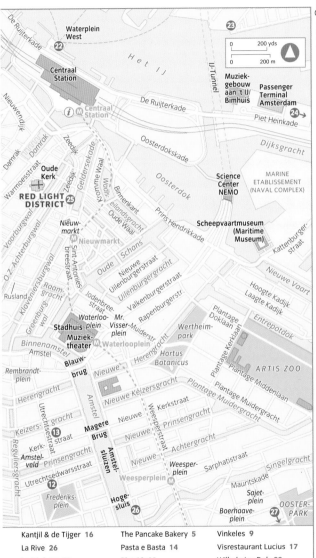

Kantjil & de Tijger 16	The Pancake Bakery 5	Vinkeles 9
La Rive 26	Pasta e Basta 14	Visrestaurant Lucius 17
Le Pêcheur 15	Pier 10 22	Wilhelmina-Dok 23
Lof 21	Supperclub 18	
Mamouche 11	Tempo Doeloe 13	ⓘ Information
Nam Kee 25	Toscanini 2	✉ Main Post Office
		Ⓜ Metro

Amsterdam Restaurants A to Z

★ Albatros Seafoodhouse

JORDAAN *SEAFOOD* The Atlantic and North Sea fish served here are grilled, poached, and fried in the simplest manner, then served in ship-ahoy decor (or on a sidewalk terrace) by friendly old-timers in a relaxed neighborhood atmosphere. Try the mixed seafood salad, the raw herring, or the sea bass. Reservations recommended. *Westerstraat 264 (at Lijnbaansgracht).* ☎ *020/627-9932. www.restaurantalbatros.nl. Entrees 13€–23€. AE, DC, MC, V. Dinner Thurs–Mon. Tram: 3 or 10 to Marnixplein. Map p 92.*

★ Bloesem

OLD CENTER *FUSION* Hip and elegant, Bloesem serves up an unusual brand of cuisine: European fusion, with offerings such as garlic soup with chorizo, duck confit with sauerkraut, or a Belgian endive salad with Valencia oranges. *Binnen Dommersstraat 13–15 (at Vinkenstraat).* ☎ *020/770-0407. www. restaurant-bloesem.nl. Entrees 16€– 22€; fixed-price menus 33€–43€. AE. Dinner Tues–Sun. Tram: 3 to Haarlemmerplein. Map p 92.*

★★ Bordewijk

JORDAAN *FRENCH FUSION* Trendy, affluent locals and laid-back gourmands come here for the creative French cuisine with Mediterranean and Asian accents, and the superb cheese and wine lists. There are usually a few Asian-influenced dishes and a sushi-style appetizer. In summer, you can dine alfresco. Reservations recommended. *Noordermarkt 7 (at Prinsengracht).* ☎ *020/624-3899. www.bordewijk.nl. Entrees 20€–30€; fixed-price menus 39€–54€. AE, DC, MC, V. Dinner Tues–Sat. Tram: 1, 2, 5, 13, or 17 to Martelaarsgracht. Map p 92.*

Brasserie Keyzer

MUSEUM DISTRICT *DUTCH/INTERNATIONAL* This classy, century-old restaurant with dark, dusky decor and starched pink linens serves fresh fish, hare, and venison along with the usual international favorites. *Van Baerlestraat 96 (beside the Concertgebouw).* ☎ *020/675-1866. www. brasseriekeyzer.nl. Entrees 23€– 33€; fixed-price lunch 28€; fixed-price dinner 32€–43€. AE, DC, MC, V. Breakfast, lunch & dinner daily. Tram: 3, 5, 12, 16, or 24 to Museumplein. Map p 91.*

Brasserie de Poort

OLD CENTER *DUTCH* In business since 1870,

Be sure to sample a variety of Dutch cheeses while you're in Amsterdam.

this former beer hall serves classic Dutch cuisine in a graceful, wood-paneled setting. Pea soup, lamb, and "numbered" steaks—every hundredth comes with a free bottle of wine—are the highlights. *In the Hotel Die Port van Cleve, Nieuwezijds Voorburgwal 176–180 (at the Dam).* ☎ *020/714-2930. www. dieportvancleve.com. Entrees 20€–30€; fixed-price menus 33€–35€. AE, DC, MC, V. May–Oct lunch & dinner daily; Nov–Apr lunch Thurs–Sun, dinner Fri–Sat. Tram: 1, 2, 5, 13, 14, or 17 to the Dam. Map p 92.*

Café-Restaurant Van Puffelen CANAL BELT *INTERNATIONAL* This brown café has grown to be a restaurant that rambles through several canal houses. It serves dishes with a creative flair, based mainly around Continental and Asian originals. Food is served until midnight. *Prinsengracht 377 (at Reestraat).* ☎ *020/624-6270. www.goodfoodgroup.nl. Entrees 16€–19€; fixed-price menu 21€. Lunch Fri–Sun; dinner daily. Tram: 13, 14, or 17 to Westermarkt. Map p 92.*

Caffepc MUSEUM DISTRICT/VONDELPARK *INTERNATIONAL* Smack dab in the middle of Amsterdam's most elegant shopping street, you can take your place among the fabulous models and fashion gurus and sip on a martini while indulging in tapas and fresh salads. *Pieter Cornelisz Hooftstraat 87 (at Van de Veldestraat).* ☎ *020/673-4752. www.unlimitedlabel.com. Entrees 14€–20€. AE, DC, MC, V. Breakfast, lunch & dinner daily (closes Sun–Wed 7pm, Thurs 10pm, Fri–Sat 8pm). Tram: 2 or 5 to Hobbemastraat. Map p 91.*

★★ **Christophe** CANAL BELT *FRENCH/MEDITERRANEAN* Ultra refined but with a modern flair best describes the cuisine at French chef Jean-Joel Bonsens's elegant restaurant. On a menu that changes

seasonally, North African and Italian elements find a place alongside French staples. *Leliegracht 46 (at Keizersgracht).* ☎ *020/625-0807. www.restaurantchristophe.nl. Reservations required. Entrees 29€–46€; fixed-price menus 36€–66€. AE, MC, V. Dinner Tues–Sat. Tram: 13, 14, or 17 to Westermarkt. Map p 92.*

★ **De Belhamel** CANAL BELT *CONTINENTAL* If you score a window table in the Art Nouveau–style dining room, you'll have a terribly romantic view of the junction of two canals. The eclectic menu changes often and covers meat (look for game options in fall and winter), fish, and vegetarian dishes. In summer, you can dine on a sidewalk terrace. *Brouwersgracht 60 (at Herengracht).* ☎ *020/622-1095. www.belhamel.nl. Entrees 13€–25€; fixed-price menus 36€–42€. AE, MC, V. Lunch & dinner daily. Tram: 1, 2, 5, 13, or 17 to Martelaarsgracht. Map p 92.*

★ **De Duvel** DE PIJP *INTERNATIONAL* Packed with hip and trendy locals, De Duvel (the Devil) serves excellent food in a cozy red dining room. Peanut-pumpkin soup and mushrooms filled with snails are some of the more daring dishes. You'll also find a daily selection of pasta, seafood, and chicken offerings. *Eerste Van der Helststraat 59–61 (at Gerard Doustraat).* ☎ *020/675-7517. www.deduvel.nl. Entrees 13€–18€. AE, DC, MC, V. Lunch Tues–Sun; dinner daily. Tram: 16 or 24 to Albert Cuypstraat. Map p 92.*

★★ **De Kas** AMSTERDAM SOUTH *INTERNATIONAL* In summer, the huge outdoor patio seats more than 100 guests adjacent to fragrant herb gardens. The interior is light and spacious (it was formerly a greenhouse), beneath a tented glass ceiling. You get just a couple of variations on a three-course fixed menu that changes daily, and the chef

The Best Dining

Stop for a cup of coffee or a beer at De Prins.

makes extensive use of organic products and ingredients. Reservations recommended. *Kamerlingh Onneslaan 3 (at Park Frankendael).* ☎ *020/462-4562. www.restaurant dekas.nl. Fixed-price lunch 38€; fixed-price dinner 50€ (chef's table 125€). AE, DC, MC, V. Lunch Mon–Fri; dinner Mon–Sat. Tram: 9 to Hogeweg. Map p 92.*

★ **De Prins** CANAL BELT *CONTINEN-TAL* Relax with the locals at a place that's my favorite traditional Dutch *eetcafé* (cafe with eats) in Amsterdam, just across the canal from the Anne Frankhuis. Select from an unpretentious but inventive menu, and choose from a great selection of Dutch and Belgian beers. *Prinsengracht 124 (at Egelantiersgracht).* ☎ *020/624-9382. www.deprins.nl. Entrees 12€–18€. AE, DC, MC, V. Lunch & dinner daily. Tram: 13, 14, or 17 to Westermarkt. Map p 92.*

★★ **Fifteen Amsterdam** WATER-FRONT *CONTINENTAL* London celebrity chef Jamie Oliver's hot spot has drop-dead gorgeous staff, clientele, and food. Though Oliver rarely presides in person, his signature breezy yet professional approach permeates both the service and the

fusiony Mediterranean cuisine, in a setting that artfully combines grafitti, sheet metal, and polished-wood tables. *Pakhuis Amsterdam, Jollemanhof 9 (at Oostelijke Handels-kade).* ☎ *020/509-5015. www.fifteen. nl. Reservations recommended. Entrees 17€–23€. AE, MC, V. Lunch Mon–Sat; dinner daily. Tram: 10 or 26 to Rietlandpark. Map p 92.*

Golden Temple CANAL BELT *VEGETARIAN* This is one of the best vegetarian (and vegan) options in town. Although the minimalist atmosphere is a tad too hallowed, the menu livens things up, with its unlikely roster of Indian and Middle Eastern plates, and Italian pizza. Mixed platters are a good way to go. *Utrechtsestraat 126 (2 blocks south of Prinsengracht).* ☎ *020/626-8560. www.restaurantgoldentemple. com. Pizza 8€–12€; mixed platter 16€–19€. MC, V. Tues–Sat lunch; dinner daily. Tram: 4 to Prinsengracht. Map p 92.*

★ **Kantjil & de Tijger** OLD CEN-TER *INDONESIAN* Unlike Holland's many Indonesian restaurants that wear their ethnic origins on their sleeves, with staffers decked out in traditional costume, the Antelope and the Tiger is chic and modern. A bestseller in this popular eatery is the 20-item rijsttafel for two. Reservations recommended for Friday and Saturday evening. *Spuistraat 291–293 (at Spui).* ☎ *020/620-0994. www.kantjil.nl. Entrees 13€–16€; rijsttafels 43€–55€ for 2. AE, MC, V. Dinner Mon–Fri; lunch & dinner Sat–Sun. Tram: 1, 2, or 5 to Spui. Map p 92.*

★★ **LAB111** VONDELPARK *DUTCH/ CONTINENTAL* This self-described "media cafe" occupies the unlikely setting of a former pathology laboratory that now houses the SMART Project Space avant-garde arts center. The restaurant's cool black-and-metal look is perked up by flashes of electric color. The menu offers Dutch and Mediterranean cuisine. *Arie Biemondstraat 111 (at Jacob van Lennepkade).* ☎ *020/616-9994. www.lab111.nl. Entrees 15€–20€; fixed-price menu 15€. AE, MC, V. Lunch Mon–Sat; dinner daily. Tram: 7 or 17 to Ten Katestraat. Map p 91.*

★★★ **La Rive** OOST *FRENCH/ MEDITERRANEAN* Service at the city's top-rated restaurant, helmed by master chef Rogér Rassin, can be as stiff as the ironed linens. Nevertheless, you'll dine like royalty on specials like Bresse pigeon with pistachio and corn, or the grill-roasted rack of lamb with dates and Zaanse mustard. Reservations required. *In the Amstel InterContinental Hotel, Professor Tulpplein 1 (off Weesperstraat).* ☎ *020/520-3264. www. restaurantlarive.nl. Entrees 57€–80€; fixed-price lunch 49€; fixed-price dinner 90€–112€. AE, DC, MC, V. Lunch Mon–Fri; dinner Mon–Sat. Tram: 7 or 10 to Sarphatistraat. Map p 92.*

★★ **Le Garage** MUSEUM DISTRICT *FUSION* The hottest restaurant in town serves up creative fusion dishes (such as white tuna with a pepper crust and a spicy Indonesian sauce) in a setting with bright lights and big mirrors that's reminiscent of Las Vegas or Tokyo. *Ruysdaelstraat 54–56 (at Van Baerlestraat).* ☎ *020/ 679-7176. www.restaurantlegarage. nl. Reservations recommended. Entrees 25€–33€; fixed-price lunch 25€; fixed-price menus 35€–50€. AE, DC, MC, V. Lunch Mon–Fri; dinner daily. Tram: 3, 5, 12, or 24 to Roelof Hartplein. Map p 91.*

★ **Le Pêcheur** OLD CENTER *SEAFOOD* The focus in this airy, tranquil restaurant is less on presentation and more on freshness and taste. Come here for house-smoked salmon or fresh oysters and mussels from the Dutch province of Zeeland. Extensive wine list. *Reguliersdwarsstraat 32 (behind the Flower Market).* ☎ *020/624-3121. www. lepecheur.nl. Entrees 21€–40€; fixed-price menu 40€. AE, MC, V. Lunch Mon–Fri; dinner Mon–Sat. Tram: 1, 2, or 5 to Koningsplein. Map p 92.*

★ **Lof** OLD CENTER *INTERNATIONAL* For all its unobtrusive persona and minimalist decor, Lof (the name is Dutch for "Praise") is highly commendable. The roster of dishes on offer—there's no menu—changes daily depending on what's fresh at local markets, and although the

Some of the 20-odd dishes you might find at an Indonesian rijsttafel.

The dining room at Pier 10 has great waterfront views.

choice is limited, it always includes a fish, a meat, and a vegetarian option. *Haarlemmerstraat 62.* ☎ *020/620-2997. Fixed-price menu 35€–45€. AE, MC, V. Dinner Tues–Sun. Tram: 1, 2, 5, 13, or 17 to Martelaarsgracht. Map p 92.*

★ **Mamouche** DE PIJP *MOROCCAN* You'll find innovative trans-Mediterranean cuisine—a blend of Maghreb (North African) dishes and French influences—in this neighborhood restaurant that looks something like a traditional Dutch *eetcafé*. The lamb tagine with prunes, almonds, olives, and lentils is a specialty of the house. *Quellijnstraat 104 (at Marie Heinekenplein).* ☎ *020/670-0736. www.restaurantmamouche.nl. Entrees 16€–22€. MC. Dinner daily. Tram: 16 or 24 to Stadhouderskade. Map p 92.*

Nam Kee OLD CENTER *CHINESE* Don't let the drab, neon-lit dining room dissuade you from trying the very good, fresh food here. Service is fast and they're open late, so you can dine until midnight. I love the dim sum and the roast Peking duck

with plum sauce. *Zeedijk 111–113 (at Nieuwmarkt).* ☎ *020/624-3470. www.namkee.nl. Entrees 7€–19€. No credit cards. Lunch & dinner daily. Metro: Nieuwmarkt. Map p 92.*

★ **Pasta e Basta** CANAL BELT *ITALIAN* This cozy, candlelit Italian restaurant has the best opera-singing waiters this side of La Scala. The fantastic antipasti buffet is served out of an antique grand piano, and the main courses include a delicious Gorgonzola lasagna with Parma ham and fresh basil. *Nieuwe Spiegelstraat 8 (btw. Keizersgracht & Herengracht).* ☎ *020/422-2222. www. pastaebasta.com. Entrees 14€–28€; fixed-price menus 37€–55€. AE, DC, MC, V. Dinner daily. Tram: 16, 24, or 25 to Keizersgracht. Map p 92.*

★ **Pier 10** WATERFRONT *CONTINENTAL* Perched on a pier behind Centraal Station, this restaurant has great views of Het IJ waterway and the port traffic that was once Amsterdam's lifeblood. Candlelight softens the funky diner decor, and the fanciful international-eclectic food—salads, steak, and fish—ebbs and flows like the tides in Het IJ. Reservations recommended on weekends. *De Ruyterkade, Steiger 10 (behind Centraal Station).* ☎ *020/ 427-2310. www.pier10.nl. Entrees 20€–22€. No credit cards. Dinner daily. Tram: 1, 2, 4, 5, 9, 16, 17, 24, 25, or 26 to Centraal Station. Map p 92.*

★ **Sama Sebo** MUSEUM DISTRICT/ VONDELPARK *INDONESIAN* This upmarket Indonesian restaurant is decorated with rush mats and batiks and serves an unrivaled 23-plate rijsttafel (a feast consisting of rice and many accompanying dishes like curried meats, fish, vegetables, and nuts) just a few steps from the Rijksmuseum. *Pieter Cornelisz Hooftstraat 27 (at Hobbemastraat).* ☎ *020/ 662-8146. www.samasebo.nl.*

Fixed-price lunch 16€–17€; rijsttafel 30€. AE, DC, MC, V. Lunch & dinner Mon–Sat. Tram: 2 or 5 to Hobbemastraat. Map p 91.

★ **Supperclub** OLD CENTER *FUSION* Kick back in this ultramodern, blindingly white, hypertrendy restaurant; stretch out on couches and cushions; and groove along to whatever the DJ is spinning. There's no telling what the chefs (called "food magicians") will whip up—you inform your waiter of any dietary restrictions and wait to see what arrives on your table. The atmosphere, not the food, is the highlight here. Reservations required. *Jonge Roelensteeg 21*

In Amsterdam, a caffe latte (coffee with milk) is called koffie verkeerd. If you order a koffie, you'll probably get black coffee, with sugar and cream on the side.

Sample various Indonesian dishes with the rijsttafel at Tempo Doeloe.

(1 block south of the Dam). ☎ 020/344-6400. www.supperclub.nl. *Fixed-price menus 65€–70€. AE, DC, MC, V. Dinner daily. Tram: 1, 2, 5, 13, 14, or 17 to the Dam. Map p 92.*

★★ **Tempo Doeloe** CANAL BELT *INDONESIAN* For authentic Indonesian cuisine, this place is hard to beat. It has a restrained ambience yet serves its dishes on fine china. There are three different rijsttafel options, including the 15-plate vegetarian *sayoeran,* the 15-plate *stimoelan, and* the sumptuous 25-plate *istemewa.* For great individual dishes, try the *nasi koening* or any of the vegetarian options. Reservations required. *Utrechtsestraat 75 (btw. Prinsengracht & Keizersgracht).* ☎ 020/625-6718. www.tempodoeloe restaurant.nl. *Entrees 14€–25€; rijsttafel 28€–36€; fixed-price menu 27€–45€. AE, DC, MC, V. Dinner daily. Tram: 4 to Keizersgracht. Map p 92.*

kids **The Pancake Bakery** CANAL BELT *PANCAKES* A 17th-century canal warehouse is home to this simple eatery where you can sample yummy pancakes with all kinds of toppings, from curried turkey with pineapple to honey, nuts, and whipped cream. *Prinsengracht 191 (at Prinsenstraat).* ☎ 020/625-1333. www.pancake.nl. *Pancakes 5€–14€. AE, MC, V. Lunch & dinner daily. Tram: 13, 14, or 17 to Westermarkt. Map p 92.*

★ **Toscanini** JORDAAN *ITALIAN* This charming eatery has an open kitchen and the unembellished country-style decor is flooded with natural light from skylights during the day. Authentic Italian dishes include veal lasagna, seafood risotto, a selection of fresh fish, and many excellent pastas. *Lindengracht 75 (off Brouwersgracht).* ☎ *020/623-2813. www.toscanini.nu. Entrees 12€–27€; fixed-price menu 45€. AE, MC, V. Dinner Mon–Sat. Tram: 3 to Willemsstraat. Map p 92.*

★★ **Vinkeles** CANAL BELT *FRENCH* This place in the atmospheric setting of a 17th-century almshouse's converted bakery is ultrachic and ultrahip. Top chef Dennis Kuipers whips up dishes such as roasted Anjou pigeon with spices and dried apricots. Reservations recommended. *In the Dylan Hotel, Keizersgracht 384 (at Runstraat).* ☎ *020/530-2010. www.vinkeles.com. Entrees 21€–42€; fixed-price menus 70€–105€. AE, DC, MC, V. Dinner Mon–Sat. Tram: 1, 2, or 5 to Spui. Map p 92.*

Visrestaurant Lucius OLD CENTER *SEAFOOD* A solid choice for fresh seafood, Lucius offers oysters and lobsters imported from Norway and Canada. The spectacular seafood platter includes mussels, oysters, clams, shrimp, and a half lobster. *Spuistraat 247 (near Spui).* ☎ *020/624-1831. www.lucius.nl. Entrees 19€–27€; fixed-price menu 38€. AE, DC, MC, V. Dinner daily. Tram: 1, 2, or 5 to Spui. Map p 92.*

Wildschut MUSEUM DISTRICT *INTERNATIONAL* Wildschut is great any time of day, but especially on summer evenings when the large terrace is open. You'll find vegetarian lasagna, large salads, and good sandwiches here, but the people-watching is maybe more interesting than the food. *Roelof Hartplein 1–3 (off Van Baerlestraat).* ☎ *020/676-8220. www.goodfoodgroup.nl.*

The glass-walled terrace at Wilhelmina-Dok.

Entrees 15€–18€. AE, DC, MC, V. Breakfast, lunch & dinner daily. Tram: 3, 5, 12, or 24 to Roelof Hartplein. Map p 91.

★★ kids **Wilhelmina-Dok** WATERFRONT *CONTINENTAL* With its glass-walled terrace right on the ship channel, this fun cafe-restaurant boasts incredible views of passing boats and the cruise-ship terminal on the south shore. Browse the Mediterranean buffet or launch into a seafood dish from the main menu. The views and a children's menu should keep kids happy. *Nordwal 1 (at IJplein).* ☎ *020/632-3701. www.wilhelmina-dok.nl. Entrees 17€–28€; fixed-price menu 28€. AE, DC, MC, V. Lunch & dinner daily. Ferry: IJpleinveer (IJplein Ferry) to Amsterdam-Noord, then walk east a short way along the dike. Map p 92.* ●

Nightlife Best Bets

Best **Place to Sip Wine with the Young & the Beautiful**
★ Bubbles & Wines, *Nes 37 (p 106)*

Best **Place to Drink with the Locals**
Café Nol, *Westerstraat 109 (p 106)*

Friendliest **Gay Bar**
★ Amstel Fifty Four, *Amstel 54 (p 109)*

Best **Irish Pub**
O'Donnell's, *Ferdinand Bolstraat 5 (p 110)*

Dance Club That's Most **Worth a Taxi Ride**
★★ ToNight, *'s-Gravesandestraat 51 (p 109)*

Best **Brown Café with a Summer Terrace**
★ Café De II Prinsen, *Prinsenstraat 27 (p 107)*

Best **Place to Dance if You're Looking for Exclusivity**
★ Jimmy Woo, *Korte Leidsedwarsstraat 18 (p 108)*

Most **Hip & Happening Dance Club**
★★ Panama, *Oostelijke Handelskade 4 (p 108)*

Best **for Romance**
★ Chocolate Bar, *Eerste Van der Helststraat 62A (p 106)*

Hottest **Gay Dance Club**
Club FUXXX, *Warmoesstraat 96 (p 109)*

Best **Low-Key Gay Watering-Hole**
Amstel Fifty Four, *Amstel 54 (p 109)*

Best **Lesbian Bar**
★ Vivelavie, *Amstelstraat 7 (p 110)*

Best **House-Brewed Beer**
★ In de Wildeman, *Kolksteeg 3 (p 107)*

Best **Place for a Drink after Midnight**
★★ Panama, *Oostelijke Handelskade 4 (p 108)*

Best **Happy Hour**
Hoppe, *Spui 18–20 (p 107)*

Previous page: Sample a Dutch beer at a friendly cafe or bar, like Hoppe. This page: Heineken is a popular Dutch beer.

De Pijp Nightlife

Café Kale de Grote **2**

Chocolate Bar **4**

Helden **3**

O'Donnell's **1**

0	200 yds
0	200 m

Central Amsterdam Nightlife

Jacob Catskade
Kattenloot
Kostverlorenvaart
Eerste Marnix-plantsoen
Palmstraat
Willemsstraat
Brouwersgracht
Haarlemmer Houttuinen
Haarlemmerstraat
Goudsbloemstraat
Lindengracht
Noorderkerk
Frederik Hendrikplantsoen
JORDAAN
Marnixstraat
Lijnbaansgracht
Van Oldenbarneveldt-plein
Westerstraat
Anjeliersstr.
Prinsengracht
Prinsen-straat
Keizers-gracht
Heren-straat
Heren-gracht
Singel
Frederik Hendrik str.
Egelantiersstraat
Egelantiersgracht
Nassaukade
Singelgracht
Nieuwe Leliestraat
Lellegracht
Spuistraat
Voorburgwal
Nieuwendijk
Tweede Hugo de Grootstraat
Bloemgracht
Westerkerk
Raadhuisstraat
Beurs-
Nieuwe Kerk
Hugo de Grootgracht
Bloemstraat
Rozengracht
Koninklijk Paleis
Dam
Nieuwezijds Voorburgwal
De Clercqstraat
Rozenstraat
Reestraat
Hartenstraat
Herengracht
Paleisstr.
Laurierstraat
Lauriergracht
Lijnbaansgracht
Keizersgracht
Prinsengracht
Kalverstraat
Rokin
Nes
Da Costastraat
Elandsstraat
Elandsgracht
Berenstraat
Wolvenstraat
Singel
Spuistraat
Nieuwe Doelenstraat
Kinkerstraat
Da Costagracht
Nassaukade
Marnixstraat
Looiersgracht
Run-straat
Huidenstraat
Spui
Heiligeweg
Rokin
Munt-plein
Jacob van Lennepkanaal
Singelgracht
Koningsplein
Herengracht
Singel
Reguliersdwarsstr.
Eerste Constantijn Huygensstr.
Leidsegracht
Leidsestraat
Kerkstraat
Keizersgracht
Vijzelstraat
Overtoom
Vondelstraat
Korte
Leidse-plein
Lange Leidsedwarsstraat
Leidsedwarsstraat
Prinsengracht
Nieuwe Spiegelstraat
Kerkstraat
Vijzelgracht
Noorderstr.
VONDELPARK
Vossiusstraat
Pieter Cornelisz Hooftstraat
Stadhouderskade
Hobbemastraat
Lijnbaansgracht
Weteringschans
Weteringstraat
Eerste Wetering dwarsstr.
Rijksmuseum
Singelgracht
Vijzelgracht
Wetering-plantsoen

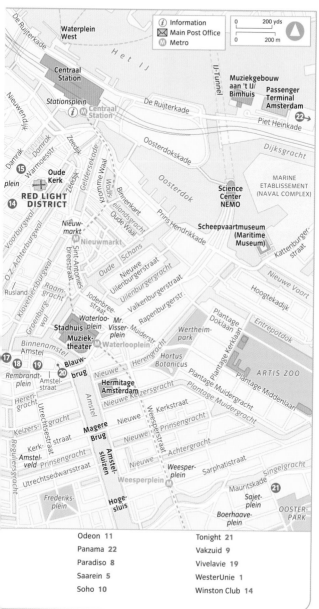

Nightlife A to Z

You can meet Amsterdammers at a canalside cafe or bar.

Bars

★ **Bubbles & Wines** OLD CENTER Just a few minutes' walk from the Dam, this fancy champagne and wine bar—all subdued lighting, dark wood surfaces, and red tones—serves an extensive roster of champagne and wine labels, along with light snacks. *Nes 37 (at Pieter Jacobszstraat).* ☎ *020/422-3318. www.bubblesand wines.com. Tram: 4, 9, 14, 16, 24, or 25 to the Dam. Map p 104.*

★★ **Cafe Kale de Grote** DE PIJP Soft chairs, long banquettes, and chandeliers draw a hip, youthful crowd to sip mojitos and other cocktails, graze on plates of tempura, and dance to DJs on Friday and Saturday nights. *Marie Heinekenplein 33 (at Ferdinand Bolstraat).* ☎ *020/ 670-4661. www.cafekale.nl. Tram: 16 or 24 to Stadhouderskade. Map p 103.*

Café Nol JORDAAN This cafe is more like a relaxed bar. It caters to a mix of young, cool Jordaaners and old-timers who have lived in the neighborhood for ages. The kitsch interior includes crystal chandeliers, mirrors, a red carpet, and hanging potted plants. *Westerstraat 109 (near Noordermarkt).* ☎ *020/624-5380. www.cafenolamsterdam.nl. Tram: 3 or 10 to Marnixplein. Map p 104.*

★ **Chocolate Bar** DE PIJP A hip hangout with a sparse 1970s retro look, this smooth place serves up spiffy cocktails and more-than-decent light meals. DJs spin great music Thursday through Saturday, and there's a terrace for when the weather's fine. *Eerste Van der Helst-straat 62A (at Govert Flinckstraat).* ☎ *020/675-7672. www.chocolate-bar.nl. Tram: 16 or 24 to Albert Cuypstraat. Map p 103.*

★★ **De Jaren** OLD CENTER On the Binnenamstel waterfront, this postmodern spot is big and sunny, with a panoramic upper-floor terrace where the young and hip lounge in sweet anonymity. There's a great salad bar, soups, and good daily quiches, and a separate restaurant. *Nieuwe Doelenstraat 20–22 (at Muntplein).* ☎ *020/625-5771. www. cafe-de-jaren.nl. Tram: 4, 9, 14, 16, 24, or 25 to Muntplein. Map p 104.*

★ **Helden** DE PIJP A young well-heeled crowd sinks into the sofas and sips martinis and mojitos over soft music at this trendy place. The food's good too, and there's a pleasant summer terrace where you can lounge alfresco. *Eerste Van der Helst-straat 42 (at Marie Heinekenplein).* ☎ *020/673-3332. www.helden.nu. Tram: 16 or 24 to Stadhouderskade. Map p 103.*

from young backpackers to middle-aged professionals. *Prinsenstraat 27.* ☎ *020/624-9722. Tram: 1, 2, 5, 13, or 17 to Martelaarsgracht. Map p 104.*

Hoppe OLD CENTER This historic brown café, dating back to 1670, has a convivial, smoky atmosphere. It's often crowded, especially with the after-work crowd, so expect standing room only in the early evenings. It gets boisterous here when the professionals leave. *Spui 18–20.* ☎ *020/420-4420. www.cafe-hoppe. nl. Tram: 1, 2, or 5 to Spui. Map p 104.*

★ **In de Wildeman** OLD CENTER This historic brown café dates back to 1690 and has its original tile floor and rows of bottles from when it functioned as a distillery. It boasts 17 draft and 200 bottled beers from around the world. It's a laid-back atmosphere, with mostly hard-drinking but very friendly locals ranging from 30- to 50-something. *Kolksteeg 3 (at Nieuwendijk).* ☎ *020/638-2348. www. indewildeman.nl. Tram: 1, 2, 5, 13, or 17 to Nieuwezijds Kolk. Map p 104.*

Order a colaatje pils (co-la-che pilss) if you want beer in a small glass, or a bakkie or vaas if you'd like a large.

A friendly neighborhood brown café, like Café De Il Prinsen, can be a great place to mix with locals.

★ **Lux** LEIDSEPLEIN Although the Leidseplein area is quite touristy, laid-back Lux draws in a healthy dose of locals with its chic attitude. Sit on the upper level to enjoy a sweeping view of the place. *Marnixstraat 403 (at Leidsegracht).* ☎ *020/422-1412. www.hotelweber.nl. Tram: 1, 2, 5, 7, or 10 to Leidseplein. Map p 104.*

★ **Vakzuid** ZUID Located inside the Olympic Stadium used for the 1928 Games, this chic cocktail bar, lounge, restaurant, and club evokes the interior design of that period in an updated form, and has a large canalside terrace. *Olympisch Stadion 35 (at Stadionplein).* ☎ *020/570-8400. www.vakzuid.nl. Tram: 16 or 24 to Stadionplein. Map p 104.*

Brown Cafés
★ **Café De Il Prinsen** CANAL BELT The "Two Princes"—in Dutch, De Twee Prinsen—an attractive brown café, has mosaic-tiled floors and a wood-muraled ceiling. I like to while away a warm evening on the summer terrace overlooking Prinsengracht. There's usually a healthy mix of local intellectuals and visitors,

Dance Clubs

Club Home REMBRANDTPLEIN
This ultratrendy place tends to attract Dutch celebs (and wannabes) and offers a variety of music on its three floors, depending on the night—but the main deal here is house music. *Wagenstraat 3 (at the Amstel).* ☎ *020/620-1375. www.clubhome.nl. Cover 10€–12€. Tram: 4, 9, or 14 to Rembrandtplein. Map p 104.*

★★ **Escape** REMBRANDTPLEIN
Three dance floors, a great sound system, and a healthy mix of local and international DJs make this one of the prime choices for the young and trendy. *Rembrandtplein 11.* ☎ *020/622-1111. www.escape.nl. Cover 10€–20€. Tram: 4, 9, or 14 to Rembrandtplein. Map p 104.*

★ **Jimmy Woo** LEIDSEPLEIN This antique-looking, Hong Kong–style club attracts a slow-burning crowd, but the music gets spikier and the vibes begin to smolder the later it gets. This spot can be hard to get into. *Korte Leidsedwarsstraat 18 (at Leidsestraat).* ☎ *020/626-3150. www.jimmywoo.com. Cover 10€–20€. Tram: 1, 2, 5, 7, or 10 to Leidseplein. Map p 104.*

★ **Odeon** CANAL BELT   Inside this 17th-century canal house converted into a multi-function venue, you'll find period ceiling paintings and stucco decor. The dance floor offers a changing palette of music styles on different nights. *Singel 460 (at Koningsplein).* ☎ *020/521-8555. www.odeontheater.nl. Cover 8€–16€. Tram: 1, 2, or 5 to Koningsplein. Map p 104.*

★★ **Panama** WATERFRONT   A historic 1899 building that used to be a power station houses this hip club. The attractive bar/restaurant in the lobby opens up into the cavernous club, which hosts big-name DJs and special events, depending on the day and seasons. This is a see-and-be-seen place for 30- to 40-something professionals. So dress to impress and bring some attitude. *Oostelijke Handelskade 4 (at Rietlandpark).* ☎ *020/311-8686. www.panama.nl. Cover 10€–25€. Tram: 10 or 26 to Rietlandpark. Map p 104.*

Paradiso LEIDSEPLEIN   An old church has been transformed into this majestic club, with lofty ceilings and high balconies encircling the dance floor. Big-name DJs and theme nights help make this place appealing to a

Brown Cafés

A friendly neighborhood *bruine kroeg* (brown café) can be a great place to mix with locals. A lot of Amsterdammers start their day at their favorite brown café, have lunch there, and then go back to socialize after dark. The brown café gets its name because of the centuries-old tobacco stains that have dyed the walls brown. They embody *gezelligheid* (coziness), and seem to evoke a bygone era. Brown cafés often open between 8 and 10am and close between 1 and 3am. They're found all over town. The standard menu features a selection of small bun sandwiches *(broodjes)* made with everything from *Amsterdamse osseworst* (smoked beef sausage) to cheese, vegetables, and salami; *toost* (toasted white bread) with ham and cheese, smoked eel, or beef tartare; and a variety of simple salads.

Museum District **A&E**

Concertgebouw 1

Vondelpark
Openluchttheater 2

Central Amsterdam **A&E**

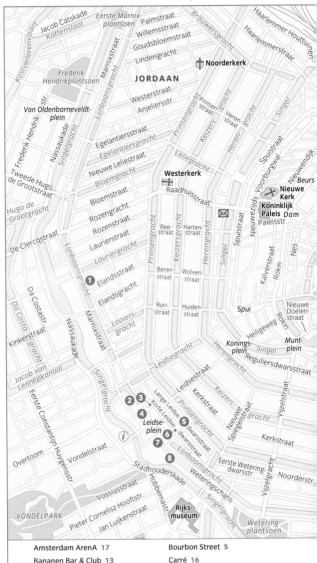

Amsterdam ArenA **17**	Bourbon Street **5**
Bananen Bar & Club **13**	Carré **16**
Beurs van Berlage **10**	Casa Rosso **14**
Bimhuis **12**	De Balie **7**
Boom Chicago **3**	EYE Film Instituut Nederland **9**

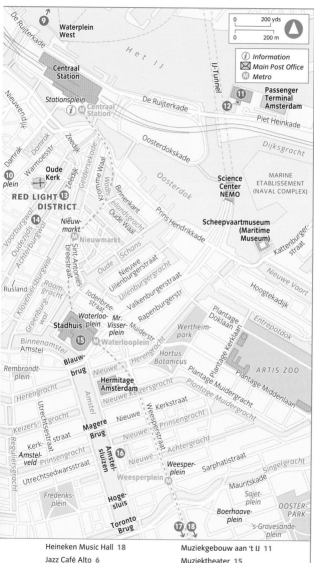

Heineken Music Hall 18	Muziekgebouw aan 't IJ 11
Jazz Café Alto 6	Muziektheater 15
Maloe Melo 1	Paradiso 8
Melkweg 2	Stadsschouwburg 4

Arts & Entertainment A to Z

An improv performance at Boom Chicago.

Classical Music

★ **Beurs van Berlage** OLD CENTER The former home of the Amsterdam Stock Exchange, an architectural marvel from 1903 designed by Hendrik Petrus Berlage, is now a congress and sometimes concert venue with two halls. The venue accommodates visiting symphony orchestras and chamber orchestras. *Beursplein 1 (at the Dam).* ☎ *020/531-3350. www.beurs vanberlage.nl. Tickets 15€–25€. Tram: 4, 9, 14, 16, 24, or 25 to the Dam. Map p 114.*

★★★ **Concertgebouw** MUSEUM DISTRICT The home of the Royal Concertgebouw Orchestra first opened its doors in 1888 and is still touted as one of the most acoustically perfect concert halls in the world. Great orchestras, ensembles, conductors, and soloists regularly perform here. There are two halls: a main hall and a recital hall, which hosts smaller ensembles, like chamber orchestras. Each hall hosts a daily performance. *Concertgebouwplein 2–6 (at Museumplein).* ☎ *0900/671-8345. www.concertgebouw.nl. Tickets 17€–75€; Aug summer*

concerts 30€. Tram: 3, 5, 12, 16, or 24 to Museumplein. Map p 113.

Comedy Theater

★ **Boom Chicago** LEIDSEPLEIN Amsterdam's premier comedy theater has been going strong since 1993, with lots of improvisational shows. The partly scripted, partly improvised humor takes aim at life in Amsterdam, the Dutch, tourists, and any other convenient target. Most performances are in English. *Leidseplein Theater, Leidseplein 12.* ☎ *020/423-0101. www.boom chicago.nl. Tickets 19€–39€; tickets/meals/drinks packages 34€–90€. Tram: 1, 2, 5, 6, 7, or 10 to Leidseplein. Map p 114.*

Concerts

Amsterdam ArenA ZUIDOOST From sports (soccer, mostly) to big-name rock concerts, the city's biggest events take place at this giant arena, located in southeast Amsterdam. *ArenA Blvd. 1 (at Amsterdam ArenA).* ☎ *020/311-1313. www. amsterdamarena.nl. Tickets 15€–140€. Metro: Bijlmer ArenA. Map p 114.*

★ **Heineken Music Hall** ZUIDOOST   Near the giant Amsterdam ArenA, this smaller venue hosts more intimate concerts. Recent performers have included Katy Perry, Kylie Minogue, Golden Earring, and Toto. *ArenA Blvd. 590 (at Amsterdam ArenA).* ☎ *0900/687-4242. www.heineken-music-hall.nl. Tickets 30€–75€. Metro: Bijlmer ArenA. Map p 114.*

★★ **Muziekgebouw aan 't IJ** WATERFRONT   This spectacular modern glass construction, located on the IJ waterfront east of Centraal Station, is the hub of contemporary and experimental music in Amsterdam. Top local and international musicians perform here. See "Bimhuis," below. *Piet Heinkade 1 (at Veemkade).* ☎ *020/788-2000. www. muziekgebouw.nl. Tickets 10€–60€. Tram: 25 or 26 to Muziekgebouw Bimhuis. Map p 114.*

★ **Paradiso** LEIDSEPLEIN   This old church has been transformed to present an eclectic variety of music. It's a great place for dance events Thursday through Sunday, and it doubles as a concert venue for big-name artists. The Rolling Stones,

Muziekgebouw aan 't IJ.

David Bowie, and Prince have all played here. *Weteringschans 6–8 (at Max Euweplein).* ☎ *020/626-4521. www.paradiso.nl. Tickets 10€–22€. Tram: 1, 2, 5, 7, or 10 to Leidseplein. Map p 114.*

Vondelpark Openluchttheater MUSEUM DISTRICT   This open-air venue comes to life on certain nights from June through August, when pop, rock, Latin, or classical

Vondelpark Openluchttheater.

Members of the Netherlands Opera perform Elektra *at the Muziektheater.*

artists give free concerts in the midst of peaceful, green Vondelpark. Bring a picnic and enjoy an enchanting evening under the stars. *Vondelpark (center of park, at Grote Vijver pond).* ☎ *020/428-3360. www.openluchttheater.nl. Free admission. Tram: 1, 2, 5, 7, or 10 to Leidseplein. Map p 113.*

Dance & Opera

★★★ **Muziektheater** WATER-LOOPLEIN   One of the city's stellar performance venues, this place has a superbly equipped 1,600-seat auditorium and is the home base of both the highly regarded Netherlands Opera and the National Ballet. The acclaimed Netherlands Dance Theater, based in The Hague, also performs here regularly. *Waterlooplein 22 (theater entrance Amstel 3).* ☎ *020/625-5455. www.het-muziek theater.nl. Tickets 17€–100€. Tram: 9 or 14 to Waterlooplein. Map p 114.*

Film

De Balie LEIDSEPLEIN   This all-purpose cultural center has an eclectic calendar of workshops, lectures, and film festivals. You can see controversial and award-winning features and documentaries and lots of interesting movies from around the world that don't make it to mainstream theaters. *Kleine-Gartmanplantsoen 10 (at Max Euweplein).* ☎ *020/553-5151. www.debalie.nl. Movie tickets*

8€; lectures 6€–10€. Tram: 1, 2, 5, 7, or 10 to Leidseplein. Map p 114.*

★ **EYE Film Instituut Nederland** WATERFRONT   Much more than just a film museum, this art cinema is due to move in 2012 from its old location in Vondelpark to a new, striking modern building in Amsterdam-Noord (North). It holds four theaters that schedule interesting retrospectives and film festivals. *Overhoeks (across Het IJ from Centraal Station).* ☎ *020/589-1400. www.eyefilm.nl. Tickets 8€. Ferry: Buiksloterwegveer from behind Centraal Station. Map p 114.*

Jazz

★ **Bimhuis** WATERFRONT   Next door to the Muziekgebouw aan 't IJ (see above), this is the city's premier jazz, blues, and improvisational venue. *Piet Heinkade 3 (at Veemkade).* ☎ *020/788-2188. www.bimhuis.nl. Tickets 10€–30€. Tram: 25 or 26 to Muziekgebouw Bimhuis. Map p 114.*

Bourbon Street LEIDSEPLEIN   In this intimate cafe, you'll find excellent local jazz, blues, soul, and funk. Well-known performers from the U.S. and Europe play here, too. This place is hopping until well after midnight. *Leidsekruisstraat 6–8 (at Prinsengracht).* ☎ *020/623-3440. www. bourbonstreet.nl. Cover 10€ for special acts. Tram: 1, 2, 5, 7, or 10 to Leidseplein. Map p 114.*

Buying Tickets

The most convenient ticket outlet in the city is the **Amsterdams Uitburo (AUB) Ticketshop** located at the Stadsschouwburg, Leidseplein 26 (☎ 020/795-9950; www.amsterdamsuitburo.nl; tram: 1, 2, 5, 7, or 10). Here you can reserve and purchase tickets for any venue in town and also pick up a plethora of brochures, pamphlets, and schedules for any cultural event in Amsterdam, including film festivals and temporary exhibits at galleries and museums. There's a charge of 2€ to 5€ per ticket, but you may consider it worth the time you'll save by not having to chase down tickets on your own. Last-minute tickets may be available at half-price for some performances, after noon on the day of the performance. The office is open Monday to Friday from 10am to 7:30pm, Saturday from 10am to 6pm, and Sunday from noon to 6pm. In addition, you can purchase tickets and make reservations before leaving home via the AUB website.

If you are staying at an upmarket hotel, I suggest calling the concierge (even before you leave home) to arrange for reservations.

Jazz Café Alto LEIDSEPLEIN Top-notch jazz musicians play nightly in this small cafe, with the occasional blues band mixed in. On some Wednesday evenings, the noted local saxophonists Hans Dulfer and his daughter Candy Dulfer play. *Korte Leidsedwarsstraat 115 (at Leidsekruisstraat).* ☎ *020/626-3249. www.jazz-cafe-alto.nl. No cover. Tram: 1, 2, 5, 7, or 10 to Leidseplein. Map p 114.*

Maloe Melo JORDAAN This small club presents live blues most nights, interspersed with evenings of jazz and country, and jams on Tuesday and Thursday nights. Big-name musicians are featured occasionally as well. *Lijnbaansgracht 163 (at Lauriergracht).* ☎ *020/420-4592. www.maloemelo.nl. Cover 5€. Tram: 7, 10, or 17 to Elandsgracht. Map p 114.*

Jazz musicians performing at Bimhuis.

Lodging **Best Bets**

Best **Canal House Hotel**
★★ Estheréa $$ *Singel 303–309 (p 129)*

Best **for Bicycle Lovers**
Bicycle Hotel Amsterdam $ *Van Ostadestraat 123 (p 127)*

Best **for John Lennon Fans**
★ Hilton Amsterdam $$$ *Apollolaan 138 (p 129)*

Best **for Techies**
★ citizenM Amsterdam City $$ *Prinses Irenestraat 30 (p 127)*

Best **for Business Travelers**
★★ Renaissance Amsterdam $$$ *Kattengat 1 (p 133)*

Best **When Money Is No Object**
★★★ InterContinental Amstel Amsterdam $$$$ *Professor Tulpplein 1 (p 129)*

Best **for Affordable Minimalist Design**
★★ Arena $$ *'s-Gravesandestraat 51 (p 126)*

Best **Boutique Hotel**
★★★ The Dylan $$$$ *Keizersgracht 384 (p 128)*

Best **Location for Families**
Eden Lancaster $$ *Plantage Middenlaan 48 (p 128)*

Best **for Young Party Animals**
Winston $ *Warmoesstraat 129 (p 134)*

Best **Place to Call Home**
★ Vondelpark Museum B&B $$ *Vossiusstraat 14 (p 134)*

Best **Romantic Getaway**
★★ Pulitzer $$$$ *Prinsengracht 315–331 (p 132)*

Best **Minimalist Interior Design**
★★ Lloyd $–$$$$ *Handelskade 34 (p 130)*

Best **Affordable Hotel with Elegant Rooms**
★ Piet Hein $$ *Vossiusstraat 52–53 (p 131)*

Best **for Shopaholics**
★★ Patou $$ *Pieter Cornelisz Hooftstraat 63 (p 131)*

Best **for Cultivating the Mental Faculties**
★★ Sandton Hotel De Filosoof $$ *Anna van den Vondelstraat 6 (p 133)*

Previous page: The stylish lobby of the Renaissance Amsterdam.
This page: A suite at the Lloyd hotel.

up-and-coming Dutch designers. There's a casual bar and eatery called ToDrink, and in the old orphanage chapel is a hot nightclub, ToNight (p 109). *'s-Gravesandestraat 51 (at Mauritskade).* ☎ *020/850-2410. www.hotelarena.nl. 127 units. Doubles 89€–175€. AE, DC, MC, V. Tram: 7 or 10 to Korte 's-Graves-andestraat. Map p 124.*

kids Bicycle Hotel Amsterdam

DE PIJP Located a few blocks from the popular Albert Cuyp street market, this hotel caters to visitors who wish to explore Amsterdam on bicycles. You can rent bikes for 7.50€ per day and stable your trusty steed indoors. The guest rooms have plain but comfortable modern furnishings; some have kitchenettes and small balconies, and there are large rooms for families. There's no elevator. *Van Ostadestraat 123 (off Ferdinand Bolstraat).* ☎ *020/679-3452. www.bicyclehotel.com. 16 units. Doubles 40€–120€ w/breakfast. AE, MC, V. Tram: 3, 12, or 25 to Ceintuurbaan-Ferdinand Bolstraat.*

★ Bilderberg Hotel Jan Luyken

MUSEUM DISTRICT This charming boutique hotel is located on a leafy residential street. The attractive rooms feature a sophisticated, modern decor and are meticulously maintained. This place feels like a large, full-service hotel without the crowds. *Jan Luijkenstraat 58 (close to the Rijksmuseum).* ☎ *020/573-0730. www.janluyken.nl. 62 units. Doubles 99€–159€. AE, DC, MC, V. Tram: 2 or 5 to Hobbemastraat. Map p 123.*

★ The Bridge Hotel

OOST The riverfront location and large, simply furnished but comfortable rooms make this hotel a great value. Two airy and spacious apartments with picture windows are great for families. The full Dutch breakfast served every morning is a nice touch.

One of the ultramodern rooms at citizenM Amsterdam City.

Amstel 107–111 (near Carré). ☎ *020/623-7068. www.thebridgehotel.nl. 48 units. Doubles 100€–175€ w/breakfast. AE, DC, MC, V. Tram: 7 or 10 to Weesperplein. Map p 124.*

Budget Hotel Clemens Amsterdam

JORDAAN This recently refurbished hotel is comfortable and friendly. All of the fairly spacious "deluxe" rooms (which have bathrooms) as well as the fairly tight budget rooms (which do not have bathrooms) are bright, clean, and homey. Room nos. 7 and 8 have balconies facing the Westerkerk. The hotel occupies four floors in a steep-staired building, and there's no elevator. *Raadhuisstraat 39 (close to the Anne Frank House).* ☎ *020/624-6089. www.clemens hotel.nl. 9 units. Doubles 60€–150€. AE, MC, V. Tram: 13, 14, or 17 to Westerkerk. Map p 124.*

★ citizenM Amsterdam City

NIEUW ZUID With an ultramodern design, high-tech touch-screen remotes, and free Wi-Fi access, this could be the perfect Amsterdam abode for mobile citizens of the world. A fast-tram connection to the center of town compensates for a location in the business-orientated World Trade Center zone. *Prinses Irenestraat 30 (at Beethovenstraat).*

The Dylan Thomas suite at the Dylan hotel.

☎ 020/811-7090. www.citizenm amsterdamcity.com. 215 units. Doubles 72€–166€. AE, DC, MC, V. Tram: 5 to Prinses Irenestraat.

★★ The College Hotel MUSEUM DISTRICT   This modern boutique hotel is housed in a former school building (hence the name) that's a short walk from the major museums. Expect to see plenty of trendy 30-something European professionals here. *Roelof Hartstraat 1 (at Van Baerlestraat).* ☎ 020/571-1511. www.thecollegehotel.com. 43 units. Doubles 185€–285€. AE, DC, MC, V. Tram: 3, 5, 12, or 24 to Roelof Hartplein. Map p 123.

★★★ The Dylan CANAL BELT Amsterdam's swankiest boutique hotel is set in a 17th-century building on one of the city's most scenic canals. Modern elegance reigns here—many rooms have four-poster beds and spacious bathrooms. Each room is individually decorated with rich fabrics and bold colors. *Keizersgracht 384 (at Runstraat).* ☎ 020/ 530-2010. www.dylanamsterdam. com. 39 units. Doubles 395€–695€. AE, DC, MC, V. Tram: 1, 2, or 5 to Spui. Map p 124.

★★ Eden Amsterdam American LEIDSEPLEIN   Built in 1900, the hotel boasts Venetian Gothic and

Art Nouveau architectural features, while guest rooms are modern. Rooms are subdued, refined, and superbly furnished. Some have views of the Singelgracht canal, while others overlook kaleidoscopic Leidseplein. *Leidsekade 97 (at Leidseplein).* ☎ 020/556-3200. www.edenamsterdamamerican hotel.com. 175 units. Doubles 200€– 280€. AE, DC, MC, V. Tram: 1, 2, 5, 7, or 10 to Leidseplein. Map p 124.

Eden Hotel Amsterdam OLD CENTER   Across the Amstel from the Muziektheater (p 118), this scenically sited hotel has bright, modern rooms. Some are more spacious than others, and those with river views are the best of the bunch and the most in demand. *Amstel 144 (off Rembrandtplein).* ☎ 020/530-7878. www.edenamsterdamhotel.com. 218 units. Doubles 155€–225€. AE, DC, MC, V. Tram: 4 or 9 to Rembrandtplein. Map p 124.

kids Eden Lancaster Hotel Amsterdam OOST   A stone's throw from Artis Zoo and a short walk from the Tropenmuseum and the Botanical Gardens, this hotel is in a great location for families. The quiet neighborhood seems far from the hustle and bustle of the old center, but is just a 10-minute tram ride away. Attractive triple rooms are perfect if you're traveling with kids. *Plantage Middenlaan 48 (at Plantage Westermanlaan).* ☎ 020/535-6888. www.edenlancasterhotel.com. *91 units. Doubles 90€–175€. AE, DC, MC, V. Tram: 9 or 14 to Plantage Kerklaan. Map p 124.*

★★ **Estheréa** CANAL BELT This elegant boutique hotel, which is built within a group of neighboring 17th-century canal houses, has been owned by the same family since it opened. In the 1940s, the proprietors installed wood paneling, crystal chandeliers, and other structural additions. Wood bedsteads and dresser-desks lend warmth to the guest rooms. *Singel 303–309 (near Spui).* ☎ 020/624-5146. www.estherea.nl. *92 units. Doubles 130€–190€. AE, DC, MC, V. Tram: 1, 2, or 5 to Spui.*

★ **Hilton Amsterdam** NIEUW ZUID The infamous room no. 902 is where John Lennon and Yoko Ono had their "Bed-in for Peace" in 1969. Designers consulted Yoko when renovating the room, and it now features extensive use of natural materials. The hotel has modern facilities and a location in a leafy, almost suburban district. *Apollolaan 138 (at Breitnerstraat).* ☎ 020/710-6000. www.amsterdam.hilton.com. *277 units. Doubles 165€–350€. AE, DC, MC, V. Tram: 5 or 24 to Apollolaan. Map p 123.*

Hoksbergen CANAL BELT This attractive budget hotel is housed in a 300-year-old canal house and offers small but bright and clean rooms at affordable rates. Rooms at the front have canal views. There's no elevator. *Singel 301 (near Spui).* ☎ 020/626-6043. www.hotelhoksbergen.com. *19 units. Doubles 72€–129€ w/breakfast. AE, DC, MC, V. Tram: 1, 2, or 5 to Spui. Map p 124.*

★★★ **Hotel de l'Europe** OLD CENTER This classic luxury hotel

The rooms at the Estheréa are cozy and warm.

commands a prime riverside location. The rooms are plush, spacious, and bright, and all boast marble bathrooms. There's a stellar restaurant, Bord'Eau, and a summer terrace overlooking the Amstel. *Nieuwe Doelenstraat 2–8 (facing Muntplein).* ☎ 020/531-1777. www.leurope.nl. *111 units. Doubles 350€–650€. AE, DC, MC, V. Tram: 4, 9, 14, 16, 24, or 25 to De Munt. Map p 124.*

★★★ **InterContinental Amstel Amsterdam** OOST The grande dame of Dutch hotels is top-notch both in luxurious accommodations and superior customer service. Plush, elegant rooms come with Italian-marble bathrooms. There's a gorgeous indoor pool alongside the modern health club, with steam room and sauna. The hotel's restaurant, La Rive (p 97), is one of the best in the city. *Professor Tulpplein 1 (off Weesperstraat).* ☎ 020/622-6060. www.amsterdam.intercontinental.com. *79 units. Doubles 500€–700€. AE, DC, MC, V. Tram: 7 or 10 to Weesperplein. Map p 124.*

Keizershof CANAL BELT This four-story canal house dates to 1672. A grand piano in the hotel's lounge adds a certain stateliness to

Hotel de l'Europe.

the place. Rooms are beamed and cozy with simple, modern furnishings, but only two have private bathrooms. In summer, you can enjoy breakfast in the flower-filled courtyard. There's no elevator. *Keizersgracht 618 (at Nieuwe Spiegelstraat).* ☎ *020/622-2855. www.hotel keizershof.nl. 4 units. Doubles 75€– 125€ w/breakfast. MC, V. Tram: 16, 24, or 25 to Keizersgracht. Map p 124.*

★★ **Lloyd** WATERFRONT This historic Amsterdam School–style hotel in the up-and-coming Eastern Docklands boasts a wide variety of accommodations, from tiny rooms to impressive suites and duplexes (one even has a grand piano and a sweeping staircase). Most are outfitted by contemporary Dutch architects and designers. *Oostelijke Handelskade 34 (at IJhaven).* ☎ *020/561-3636. www.lloydhotel. com. 117 units. Doubles 95€–450€. AE, DC, MC, V. Tram: 10 or 26 to Rietlandpark. Map p 124.*

Mercure Amsterdam Arthur Frommer CANAL BELT This small, friendly hotel once owned by Arthur Frommer is tucked away on a side street behind Prinsengracht. The rooms are not huge but are stylish, with soft pastel colors. There's a cozy bar. *Noorderstraat 46 (off Vijzelgracht).* ☎ *020/622-0328. www.mercure. com. 93 units. Doubles 90€–170€. AE, DC, MC, V. Tram: 16, 24, or 25 to Prinsengracht. Map p 124.*

A Canal-House Warning

Elevators are difficult things to shoehorn into the cramped confines of a 17th-century canal house and cost more than some moderately priced and budget hotels can afford. Many simply don't have them. If lugging your old wooden sea chest up six flights of steep, narrow stairs is liable to void your life insurance, better make sure an elevator is in place and working. Should there be no such amenity, you might want to ask for a room on a low floor.

Museumzicht MUSEUM DISTRICT This basic hotel is housed in a Victorian house just across from the Rijksmuseum. Rooms are small but clean, and are decorated with an eclectic mix of antique furnishings. There's no elevator and the steps are quite steep. *Jan Luijkenstraat 22 (at Hobbemastraat).* ☎ *020/671-2954. www.hotelmuseumzicht.nl. 14 units. Doubles 65€–150€ w/breakfast. AE, DC, MC, V. Tram: 2 or 5 to Hobbemastraat. Map p 123.*

NH Grand Hotel Krasnapolsky OLD CENTER Smack in the midst of it all, the "Kras" faces the Royal Palace and is an Amsterdam landmark. The sizes and shapes of the rooms vary considerably and the upkeep on them is variable. Renovations are progressing somewhat haphazardly; be sure to ask for a newly renovated room. *Dam 9.* ☎ *020/554-9111. www.nh-hotels.com. 468 units. Doubles 159€–204€. AE, DC, MC, V. Tram: 4, 9, 14, 16, 24, or 25 to the Dam. Map p 124.*

Owl MUSEUM DISTRICT This solid bargain choice is just a few minutes' walk from Leidseplein, but in a quiet spot. Rooms are fairly compact, with oak furnishings and white-washed walls. There's a bar and a small garden, great for lounging on a warm summer day. *Roemer Visscherstraat 1 (off Stadhouderskade).* ☎ *020/618-9484. www.owl-hotel.nl. 34 units. Doubles 105€–132€ w/ breakfast. AE, DC, MC, V. Tram: 1 to Stadhouderskade. Map p 123.*

★ **Patou** MUSEUM DISTRICT Set on the city's most elegant shopping street, this small boutique hotel goes beyond offering mere style— though the minimalist design is quite innovative. Patou keeps a laserlike focus on doing good by its guests. *Pieter Cornelisz Hooftstraat 63 (at Honthorststraat).* ☎ *020/676-0232. www.hotelpatou.nl. 12 units. Doubles 175€–235€. AE, DC, MC, V. Tram: 2 or 5 to Hobbemastraat. Map p 123.*

★ **Piet Hein** MUSEUM DISTRICT Set in an Art Nouveau villa, this boutique hotel is decorated in tones of gray and black. They signify a cool, contemporary style that permeates the public spaces and most of the guest rooms. Unwind in the evenings in the relaxed bar/lounge or out on the garden terrace. *Vossiusstraat 52–53 (facing Vondelpark).* ☎ *020/662-7205. www. hotelpiethein.com. 65 units. Doubles 135€–250€ w/breakfast. AE, DC, MC, V. Tram: 3, 5, or 12 to Van Baerlestraat. Map p 123.*

The grand lobby of the InterContinental Amstel Amsterdam.

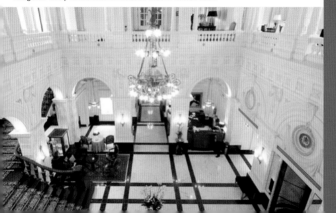

Money-Saving Tips

The Netherlands adheres to the Benelux Hotel Classification system, which awards stars to hotels based on set criteria—having a pool, an elevator, and so forth. The hotel with the most stars is not necessarily the most comfortable or elegant (though often it is). Each establishment must display a sign indicating its classification, from "1" for those with minimum amenities to "5" for deluxe, full-service hotels. Amsterdam's hotels can be expensive. If a particular hotel strikes your fancy but is out of your price range, it may pay to inquire if special off-season, weekend, specific weekday, or other packages will bring prices down to what you can afford. Many hotels offer significant rate reductions between November 1 and March 31, except during the Christmas and New Year period.

Prinsenhof CANAL BELT   This canal-house hotel offers basic but comfortable rooms with beamed ceilings. Front rooms look out onto the Prinsengracht, where colorful houseboats are moored. There's no elevator, but a pulley hauls your luggage up and down the stairs. *Prinsengracht 810 (at Utrechtsestraat).* ☎ *020/623-1772. www.hotel prinsenhof.com. 11 units. Doubles*

A sleek, minimalistic room at the Patou.

64€–89€ w/breakfast. AE, MC, V. Tram: 4 to Prinsengracht. Map p 124.

★ **Pulitzer** CANAL BELT   The Pulitzer offers its lucky guests pure luxury without being ostentatious. A superior location on a canal at the edge of the Jordaan, rooms so plush you sink into them, and a fantastic restaurant make this a good place to splurge on a romantic getaway. *Prinsengracht 315–331 (at Westermarkt).* ☎ *020/523-5235. www. pulitzeramsterdam.com. 230 units. Doubles 219€–515€. AE, DC, MC, V. Tram: 13, 14, or 17 to Westermarkt. Map p 124.*

★ **Radisson Blu** OLD CENTER   This sprawling hotel is close to everything. There are four room categories, so be sure to state your preference when you reserve. The Dutch rooms come with oak furnishings and orange curtains; the Scandinavian, Asian, and Art Deco rooms are sparser and airier. The hotel has a full restaurant and a bar that serves light meals. *Rusland 17 (at the University of Amsterdam).* ☎ *020/623-1231. www.radissonblu. com. 247 units. Doubles 150€–350€. AE, DC, MC, V. Tram: 4, 9, 14, 16, 24, or 25 to Spui. Map p 124.*

Many rooms at the Pulitzer overlook a charming canal.

★★ Renaissance Amsterdam

OLD CENTER   The Renaissance is a standout among the city's large business hotels, tucked away off a charming canal just a 5-minute walk from Centraal Station. It feels much cozier than you'd expect from its size. Rooms are very spacious, with picture windows and large bathrooms. Staff go out of their way to help. *Kattengat 1 (at Singel).* ☎ *020/621-2223. www.marriott. com. 402 units. Doubles 149€–397€. AE, DC, MC, V. Tram: 1, 2, 5, 13, or 17 to Martelaarsgracht. Map p 124.*

★★ Sandton Hotel De Filosoof

MUSEUM DISTRICT   In a quiet, leafy and upscale residential neighborhood not far from Vondelpark, you'll find this small, friendly hotel. Rooms are small but charming, and some are very bright, with large wood-framed windows. They're individually decorated in themes that reflect various philosophies (like the Golden Age–style Spinoza room, or the simply decorated Thoreau room). *Anna van den Vondelstraat 6 (off Overtoom).* ☎ *020/683-3013. www. sandton.eu. 38 units. Doubles 105€– 180€. AE, MC, V. Tram: 1 to Jan Pieter Heijestraat. Map p 123.*

★★ Seven Bridges CANAL BELT

This canal-house gem is meticulously maintained. Each individually decorated room boasts antique furnishings (Art Deco, Biedermeier, Louis XVI, rococo), handmade Italian drapes, and wood-tiled floors. Attic rooms have sloped ceilings and exposed wood beams. *Reguliersgracht 31 (at Keizersgracht).* ☎ *020/623-1329. www.sevenbridges hotel.nl. 11 units. Doubles 125€– 235€. AE, MC, V. Tram: 4 to Keizersgracht. Map p 124.*

Singel CANAL BELT

Three canal houses were united to create this bright and welcoming hotel, conveniently located near Centraal Station. A few of the modern, spacious rooms have an attractive view of the Singel canal. *Singel 13–17.* ☎ *020/626-3108. www.singelhotel.nl. 32 units. Doubles 74€–189€ w/breakfast. AE, DC, MC, V. Tram: 1, 2, 5, 13, or 17 to Martelaarsgracht. Map p 124.*

Smit MUSEUM DISTRICT

Steps from all the elegant shops on P.C. Hooftstraat, this hotel offers comfortable, if slightly small, rooms at a reasonable price. Breakfast here (not included in room rates) features delicious Gouda omelets, Dutch pancakes, and fresh croissants. *Pieter Cornelisz Hooftstraat 24–28 (at Hobbemastraat).* ☎ *020/671-4785. www.hotelsmit.com. 106 units. Doubles 104€–135€. MC, V. Tram: 2 or 5 to Hobbemastraat. Map p 123.*

Summer Stays: Reserve Ahead

July and August are tough months for finding hotel rooms in Amsterdam. Try to reserve as far ahead as possible for this period. If you have problems getting a room, contact the tourist information office, which can generally arrange a room somewhere, though it might not be in the kind of hotel you are looking for and you might need to pay more for a room in a better-class hotel.

You can reserve through (among other organizations) the **Amsterdam Tourism & Convention Board** (☎ 020/201-8800; www.iamsterdam.com).

★ **Vondelpark Museum B&B**
MUSEUM DISTRICT   The affable Fontijn family owns this 1879 mansion overlooking Vondelpark. They rent out three apartments that sleep up to four people, and one charming double bedroom on the ground floor. All units come fully equipped with antique furniture and large windows with park views; the top-floor apartment has its own private rooftop terrace. There's no elevator. *Vossiusstraat 14.* ☎ *020/676-2511. 4 units. Doubles 85€–150€ w/breakfast; apt 95€. No credit* cards. *Tram: 2 or 5 to Hobbemastraat. Map p 123.*

Winston OLD CENTER   Young partygoers flock to this vibrant budget hotel with two bars and a nightclub on the premises. It's on a somewhat seedy street, mere steps from the Red Light District. Families may want to look elsewhere, but it's a great choice for hedonists. *Warmoesstraat 129 (off Damrak).* ☎ *020/623-1380. www.winston.nl. 69 units. Doubles 69€–136€ w/breakfast. AE, DC, MC, V. Tram: 4, 9, 14, 16, 24, or 25 to the Dam. Map p 124.* ●

Rooms at the Sandton Hotel De Filosoof are individually decorated in various themes.

Haarlem

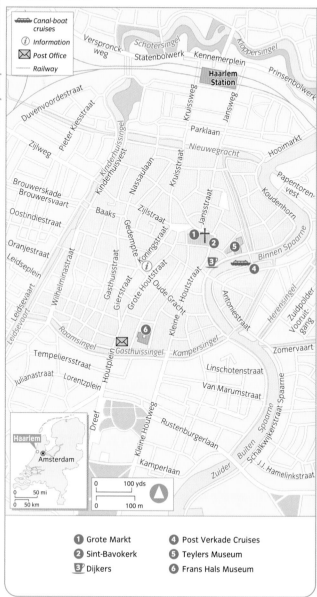

Legend
Canal-boat cruises
(i) Information
Post Office
— Railway

1. Grote Markt
2. Sint-Bavokerk
3. Dijkers
4. Post Verkade Cruises
5. Teylers Museum
6. Frans Hals Museum

Previous page: Haarlem's Sint-Bavokerk (St. Bavo's Church).

aarlem, a handsome town of 150,000 inhabitants, is where Rembrandt contemporaries Frans Hals, Jacob van Ruisdael, and Pieter Saenredam lived and painted their famous portraits, landscapes, and church interiors. Haarlem boasts one of the country's best museums and finest churches, but it has something of a traditional Dutch village feel that's typified by the lively open-air market on the main square. If you're traveling with kids, be sure to take a canal-boat cruise. **START: A straight walk of 800m (½ mile) south from Haarlem's Art Nouveau railway station, on Kruisweg, Kruisstraat, and Smedenstraat, brings you to the historic central market square.**

❶ ★★★ Grote Markt. The monumental buildings around the tree-lined square, which date from the 15th to 19th centuries, are a visual minicourse in the development of Dutch architecture. The oldest building is Haarlem's 14th-century Stadhuis (Town Hall), a former hunting lodge that was rebuilt in the 17th century. *Market Mon 8:30am–5pm; Sat 9am–5pm.*

❷ ★★ Sint-Bavokerk (St. Bavo's Church). Completed in 1520, this magnificent church—also known as the Grote Kerk (Great Church)—has a rare unity of structure and proportion. Its elegant wooden tower is covered with lead sheets and adorned with gilt spheres. The light and airy church interior has whitewashed walls and

St. Bavo's famed Christian Müller organ.

sandstone pillars. But the most fascinating feature is the soaring Christian Müller organ (1738). It has 5,068 pipes and is nearly 30m (98

Grote Markt.

Explore Haarlem's canals with a boat ride on Post Verkade Cruises.

ft.) tall. Mozart played the organ in 1766 when he was just 10 years old, and Handel and Liszt both made special visits here to play it. You can hear the organ in a free recital Tuesday at 8:15pm from May to October; in July and August, there's an additional free recital on Thursday at 4pm. From May to October, church services using the organ take place Sunday at 10am; June to September, there's an additional 7pm Vespers and Cantata service. ⏲ *45 min. Grote Markt 22.* ☎ *023/553-2040. www.bavo.nl. Admission 2.50€ adults, 1.25€ kids 12–16. July–Sept Mon–Sat 10am–5pm; Oct–May Mon–Sat 10am–4pm.*

③ ★ **Dijkers.** This tiny restaurant, popular with locals, serves hearty lunches like Thai green curry and lighter fare such as toasted sandwiches. The mozzarella and prosciutto is excellent. *Warmoesstraat 5–7 (off Oude Groenmarkt).* ☎ *023/ 551-1564. $.*

④ kids Post Verkade Cruises. A canal cruise is an ideal way to get to know Haarlem. The dock is on the Spaarne River beside the Gravenstenenbrug, a handsome lift bridge. You'll see loads of historical buildings, and pass close to an 18th-century traditional Dutch windmill—a great photo op. ⏲ *45 min. At the Spaarne River and the Gravenstenenbrug.* ☎ *023/535-7723. www.postverkadecruises.nl. Tickets 9.50€ adults, 4.50€ kids 3–12. Apr–Oct boats depart daily at noon, 1, 2, 3, and 4pm.*

⑤ kids Teylers Museum. This quirky but interesting museum was the first museum to open in the Netherlands, in 1784. It's named after the 18th-century merchant Pieter Teyler van der Hulst, who willed his entire fortune for the advancement of both art and science. You'll find a diverse collection here: drawings by Michelangelo, Raphael, and Rembrandt (which are shown in rotation); fossils, minerals, and skeletons; instruments of physics; and an odd assortment of inventions, including the largest electrostatic generator in the world (built in 1784). ⏲ *1½ hr. Spaarne 16 (at Bakenessergracht).* ☎ *023/531-9010. www.teylersmuseum.eu. 9€ adults, 2€ kids 6–17. Tues–Sat 10am–5pm; Sun & holidays noon–5pm. Closed Jan 1, Dec 25.*

⑥ ★★★ **Frans Hals Museum.** This superb museum is the highlight of many Dutch art lovers' trips to

139

Haarlem

Holland. The 1608 building was once a majestic home for retired gentlemen. Consequently, the famous paintings by Frans Hals (1580–1686) and other masters of the Haarlem School hang in settings that look like the 17th-century houses they were intended to adorn. Hals earned his living by painting portraits of members of the local Schutters (Musketeers) Guild. Typified by his *A Banquet of the Officers of the St. George Civic Guard* (1616), five such works, with a style that inspired van Gogh, hang in the museum, along with six more paintings by Hals. Among other pieces is a superb dollhouse from around 1750, and fine collections of antiques, silver, porcelain, and clocks. 🕐 *2 hr. Groot Heiligland 62 (at Gasthuisvest).* ☎ *023/511-5775. www.franshalsmuseum.com.*

Kids will love the odd inventions on display at the Teylers Museum.

Admission 10€ adults, 4.50€ ages 19–24. Tues–Sat 11am–5pm; Sun & holidays noon–5pm. Closed Jan 1 & Dec 25.

Haarlem Basics

For many Amsterdammers, Haarlem is not only the closest charming town for an afternoon of shopping at the market, but it's also home. Trains depart from Amsterdam Centraal Station for Haarlem at intervals ranging from 4 minutes to 15 minutes. The ride takes just 15 minutes, and the round-trip fare is 7.40€. Once in Haarlem, you can pretty much walk everywhere. Haarlem's Centraal Station is just a 10-minute walk from the market square and most of the attractions listed here.

For information, the city tourist office, **VVV Informatiekantoor,** Verwulft 11, 2011 GJ Haarlem (☎ **0900/616-1600;** www.haarlem marketing.nl), is in the center of town, at the intersection of Grote Houtstraat and Gedempte Oude Gracht. The office is open April to September Monday to Friday from 9:30am to 6pm, Saturday from 9:30am to 5pm, and Sunday from noon to 4pm; October to March Monday from 1 to 5:30pm, Tuesday to Friday from 9:30am to 5:30pm, and Saturday from 10am to 5pm.

Delft

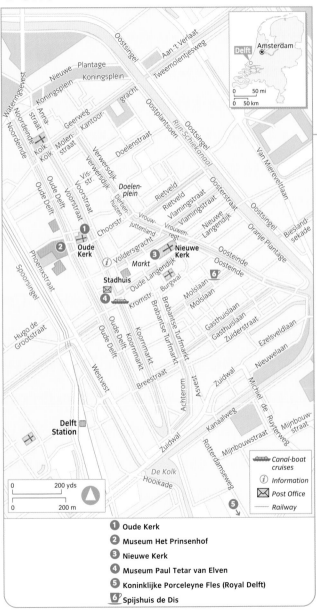

1 **Oude Kerk**
2 **Museum Het Prinsenhof**
3 **Nieuwe Kerk**
4 **Museum Paul Tetar van Elven**
5 **Koninklijke Porceleyne Fles (Royal Delft)**
6 **Spijshuis de Dis**

Delft is best known as the home of the famous blue-and-white porcelain, and on this tour you'll visit the factory where it's produced. Delft is also a small, charming city that was the cradle of the Dutch Republic, the burial place of the royal family, and the birthplace and inspiration of artist Jan Vermeer, the 17th-century master of light and subtle emotion. Take a stroll through Delft and admire the colorful flower boxes and linden trees bending over gracious canals. START: **To reach the centrally located Oude Kerk from Delft's railway station, the most scenic walking route is north along canalside Oude Delft, through the heart of the Old Town, a distance of around 800m (½ mile).**

A stained-glass window from Delft's Oude Kerk.

① ★★ **Oude Kerk (Old Church).** Vermeer's house is long gone from Delft, as are his paintings, but he's buried at the Oude Kerk. This immense 13th-century church is notable for its 27 stained-glass

windows. Also note the leaning clock tower built in the 14th century and the Gothic north transept, which was added in the 16th century by Belgian architect Anthonis Keldermans. The interior floors are paved with tomb slabs from the 17th century. ⏱ *30 min. Heilige Geestkerkhof 25 (off Oude Delft).* ☎ *015/212-3015. www. oudekerk-delft.nl. Admission (combined with Nieuwe Kerk; see below) 3.50€ adults, 3€ seniors, 2€ students 12–25, 1.50€ kids 6–11. Apr–Oct Mon–Sat 9am–6pm; Nov–Jan Mon–Fri 11am–4pm, Sat 10am–5pm; Feb–Mar Mon–Sat 10am–5pm.*

② ★★ **Museum Het Prinsenhof.** The "Father of the Nation," William I of Orange (William the Silent), lived and had his headquarters in this former convent during the years when he helped found the Dutch Republic. He was assassinated here,

Museum Het Prinsenhof.

Delft Basics

Delft is around 1 hour by train from Amsterdam. The round-trip fare is 23€. From the Delft railway station, most everything is just a 10-minute walk. For information, Delft's tourist office, the **Touristen Informatie Punt (TIP),** Hippolytusbuurt 4, 2611 HN Delft (☎ **0900/ 515-1555,** or 31-15/215-4051 from outside Holland; www.delft.nl), is in the center of town. The office is open April to September, Monday and Saturday from 10am to 5pm, Tuesday to Friday from 9am to 6pm, and Sunday from 10am to 4pm; October to March, Monday from 11am to 4pm, Tuesday to Saturday from 10am to 4pm, and Sunday from 10am to 3pm.

in 1584, and you can still see the musket-ball holes in the stairwell. Today the Prinsenhof is a museum of paintings, tapestries, silverware, and pottery. On the top floor, don't miss the accurately lit and detailed features of every militiaman's face in Michiel Jansz van Miereveld's *Civic Guard Banquet* (1611). There is also a beautiful collection of Dutch wineglasses from the 17th century. ⏱ *1 hr. Sint-Agathaplein 1 (off Phoenixstraat).* ☎ *015/260-2358.*

Delft's Nieuwe Kerk.

www.prinsenhof-delft.nl. Admission 7.50€ adults, 4€ students & kids 12–16. Tues–Sun 11am–5pm. Closed Jan 1, Easter Mon, Apr 30, Pentecost Mon & Dec 25.

❸ ★ **Nieuwe Kerk.** Prince William of Orange and other members of the House of Oranje-Nassau are buried here. The church was built between 1383 and 1510, and most of it was restored following a fire in 1536. Renowned architect PJH Cuypers added the 100m (328-ft.) tower to the Gothic facade. Architect and sculptor Hendrick de Keyser designed the ornate black-and-white marble tomb of William of Orange. After your visit to the interior, stroll around the square, admiring the church and its spire from different angles. ⏱ *30 min. Markt.* ☎ *015/212-3025. www. nieuwekerk-delft.nl. Admission: Church (combined with Oude Kerk; see above): 3.50€ adults, 3€ seniors, 2€ students 12–25, 1.50€ kids 6–11. Tower: 3.50€ adults, 3€ seniors, 2€ students 12–25, 1.50€ kids 6–11. Apr–Oct Mon–Sat 9am– 6pm; Nov–Jan Mon–Fri 11am–4pm, Sat 10am–5pm; Feb–Mar Mon–Sat 10am–5pm.*

4 Museum Paul Tetar van Elven. The 19th-century artist van Elven (1823–96) lived and worked here, and the furnishings are just as he left them. His 17th-century-style studio looks like it's ready for the artist to enter and pick up his brushes. Van Elven was a noted copyist, and a lot of his reproductions hang on the walls. Except for a subpar Vermeer on the second floor, most of them are excellent, especially the Rembrandts and the Paulus Potter on the first floor. The furniture and porcelain collections are interesting, too. *Koornmarkt 67 (south of Markt).* ☎ *015/212-4206. www.museumpaultetarvanelven.nl. Admission 4€ adults, 2€ kids 12–18. Apr–Oct Tues–Sun 1–5pm.*

5 ★ Koninklijke Porceleyne Fles (Royal Delft). If you like delftware porcelain, you'll be in heaven at the Royal Delft workshop. Not only will you get to visit the factory and get a firsthand view of the business of painting porcelain, but you can also visit the Delft museum and shop at the showroom for factory seconds at incredible bargains. But perhaps the highlight of any visit here is the workshops that teach you to paint your own porcelain, which is then fired and glazed and ready for pickup after 48 hours (or it can be shipped to your home address). The workshop cost includes the materials but not the shipping and handling costs. These workshops are available from 10am to 2:30pm, and it's advisable to call ahead for reservations. *Rotterdamseweg 196 (at Jaffalaan).* ☎ *015/251-2030. www.royaldelft.com. Tour 8€ adults, free for kids 12 and under; workshops 27€–45€. Apr–Oct daily 9am–5pm; Nov–Mar Mon–Sat 9am–5pm. Closed Jan 1, Dec 25 & 26.*

6 ★ Spijshuis de Dis. Great Dutch cooking is dished up at this atmospheric restaurant. Look for traditional plates presented in modern variations: bokkenpot (a stew made from beef, chicken, and rabbit in beer sauce), mussels prepared with garlic and spices, and more. *Beestenmarkt 36 (2 blocks east of the Markt).* ☎ *015/213-1782. Tues–Sat 5–10pm. $$.*

You can see artists at work at Delft's porcelain factory.

Rotterdam

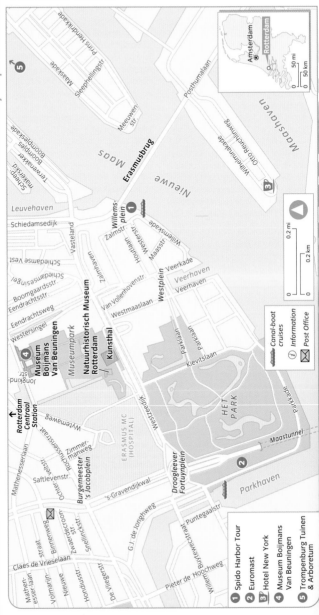

Amsterdam
Rotterdam
50 mi
50 km

Prins Hendrikkade
Maaskade
Sleephellingstr.
Meeuwen-str.
Scheepmakerskade
Terwenakker
Boompjes
Boompjeskade

Posthumalaan
Otto Reuchlinweg
Wilhelminakade

Maashaven

Erasmusbrug

Maas
Nieuwe Maas

Leuvehaven
Schiedamsedijk
Schiedamse Vest
Schiedamsesingel
Boomgaardsstr.
Eendrachtsstr.
Eendrachtsweg
Westersingel
Jonkindstr.

Vasteland
Zalmstr.
Zalmhaven
Westerstraat
Houtlaan
Willemskade
Maasstr.

1
Willems-plein

Van Vollenhovenstr.
Westmaaslaan

Westplein
Veerkade
Veerhaven

Parklaan
Kievitslaan
Parkkade

Museum Boijmans Van Beuningen **4**
Museumpark
Natuurhistorisch Museum Rotterdam
Kunsthal

← Rotterdam Centraal Station

Mathenesserlaan
Mathenesserlaan
Rochussenstraat
Zimmer-manweg
Wytemaweg
Saftlevenstr.
Ochterveltstr.
Burgemeester 's Jacobplein

ERASMUS MC (HOSPITAL)

Westzeedijk
Droogleever Fortuynplein

HET PARK
Maastunnel
Parkhaven

2

's-Gravendijkwal
Claes de Vrieselaan
Mathenesser-laan
Volmarijn-
Nieuwe
Hondiusstr.
Snellinckstr.
Zwaardecroon-
Binnenweg
De Vliegerstr.
G.J. de Jonghweg
Puntegaalstr.
Pieter de Hoochweg
Willem Buytewechstraat

Maas

3
Posthumalaan

0.2 mi
0.2 km

Canal-boat cruises
ⓘ Information
✉ Post Office

1 Spido Harbor Tour
2 Euromast
3 Hotel New York
4 Museum Boijmans Van Beuningen
5 Trompenburg Tuinen & Arboretum

Affectionately referred to as "Manhattan on the Maas" (the river that runs through it and out to the North Sea), Rotterdam was almost entirely destroyed during World War II. Its vibrant newness is part of its attraction. Rotterdam also has an important place in American history: Delfshaven, one of the only areas not wrecked during World War II, is the port from which the Pilgrim Fathers sailed to the new continent. START: **Rotterdam is a spread-out, modern city, and most of it doesn't really reward a lot of walking. You're advised to go by Metro train to Leuvehaven, or by tram even closer, to the Spido tour-boat dock on the Maas.**

1 ★ kids Spido Harbor Tours. The best way to tour Rotterdam is by taking one of the Spido line's large, comfortable boats up and down the Maas River and deep into the world's largest port. You pass under the city's most scenic landmark, the Erasmus Bridge (or Swan Bridge, as it's been dubbed by the locals), and you pass Delfshaven and its old mill (from where the pilgrims left for America in 1620). You get fabulous views of the Euromast, Rotterdam's tallest structure, built in 1960. But the most fascinating aspect of this tour is its up-close-and-personal view of the workings of this immense port: You zigzag around giant cranes, tankers, barges, and all kinds of boats and ships. Older kids and anybody with a maritime interest will love this trip. ⏱ 1¼ hr. Willemsplein 85 (under the Erasmus Bridge). ☎ 010/275-9988.

www.spido.nl. Tickets 9.75€ adults, 6€ kids 4–11. Apr–Sept departures every 30–45 min. 9:30am–5pm; Oct–Mar usually 3–4 trips per day with the last one at 3:30pm; check the website or call ahead for winter hours. Tram: 7 to Willemsplein.

2 ★★ Euromast. This slender tower, 185m (607 ft.) tall, is indisputably the best vantage point for an overall view of Rotterdam and its environs, out to 30km (19 miles) on a clear day. You can have lunch or dinner in the Euromast Brasserie, 96m (315 ft.) above the harbor park, while enjoying spectacular views of the port. A rotating elevator departs from here for the Euroscoop viewing platform. From the Brasserie level, for an additional payment (50€), you can abseil or rope slide back to the ground—definitely not for the faint of heart. *Parkhaven 20 (in Het*

Explore Rotterdam's busy port from a Spido Harbor Tours cruise.

A Grand Harbor

A dredged deepwater channel connects Rotterdam with the North Sea and forms a 40km-long (25-mile) harbor. The Port of Rotterdam is the world's third-busiest port (after Shanghai and Singapore), handling 30,000 ships and 430 million metric tons of cargo annually. You may think visiting a harbor is boring business on a vacation, but Rotterdam's is one of the most memorable sights in Holland and likely makes any other harbor you've ever seen look like a Fisher-Price toy. Container ships, bulk carriers, tankers, and care-worn tramps are waited on by a vast retinue of machines and people. Trucks, trains, and barges, each carrying its little piece of the action, hurry back and forth. Rotterdam is the pump that replenishes Europe's commercial arteries.

The bustling Port of Rotterdam.

Park). ☎ 010/436-4811. www.euromast.nl. Admission 8.90€ adults, 7.70€ seniors, 5.40€ kids 4–11. Apr–Sept daily 9:30am–11pm; Oct–Mar daily 10am–11pm. Tram: 8 to Euromast.

An exhibit at the Museum Boijmans Van Beuningen.

③ Hotel New York. The former headquarters of the Holland America shipping line is now a hotel with a lovely cafe-restaurant on its ground floor. You can take a small, wooden water taxi to get here (unless the wind is blowing too strong) from a dock at the edge of Veerkade facing the Wereldmuseum, or board tram 20, 23, or 25 from the nearby Leuvehaven stop. Once here, settle into a waterside table and enjoy large American-style salads (like Chef's or Caesar) or order from the wonderful oyster bar. *Koninginnenhoofd 1 (on Kop van Zuid).* ☎ 010/439-0500. www.hotelnewyork.nl. $$.

④ ★★ Museum Boijmans Van Beuningen. Hail a cab or take the tram to yet another of Holland's treasure-troves of fine art. Here,

you'll find walls and walls of paintings by the Dutch masters as well as works by Degas, Dalí, Man Ray, and Tintoretto. There's a fine collection of porcelain, silver, glass, and delftware, too. Don't miss Rembrandt's moving *Titus at His Desk* (1655), which depicts his son deep in thought with the gentlest play of light and shadow to portray a slightly brooding mood. Among the many distinguished objects from the 17th century is a walnut-wood clock 2m (7ft.) tall that will take your breath away. After viewing the collections, you can stroll through the tree-shaded sculpture garden and adjacent Museumpark. *Museumpark 18–20 (at Westersingel).* ☎ *010/441-9400. www.boijmans.nl. Admission 10€ adults, 5€ students, free for kids 18 and under. Tues–Sun 11am–5pm. Closed Jan 1, Apr 30 & Dec 25. Tram: 7 or 20 to Museumpark.*

⑤ ★ Trompenburg Tuinen & Arboretum. East of the center city, this city jewel has evolved from a family-owned 19th-century estate into a gorgeous garden kept in good order by an army of gardeners. Trompenburg contains more than 4,000 trees, bushes, and perennials, with oak, pine, cedar, ash, yew,

The gardens at the Trompenburg Tuinen & Arboretum provide a peaceful refuge from the busy city.

hostas, and rhododendron among those on the roster. In addition, the arboretum has a rose garden, a goldfish pond, an aviary, and a hothouse full of cacti and succulents. *Honingerdijk 86 (close to Erasmus University).* ☎ *010/233-0166. www.trompenburg.nl. Admission 5.75€ adults, free for kids 12 and under. Apr–Oct Mon–Fri 9am–5pm, Sat–Sun 10am–5pm; Nov–Mar Mon–Fri 9am–5pm, Sat 10am–4pm, Sun noon–4pm. Closed Dec 19–Jan 8 (the closed dates might vary by a few days). Tram: 7 or 21 to Woudestein.*

Rotterdam Basics

Up to 10 trains per hour depart from Amsterdam's Centraal Station for Rotterdam Centraal Station. On NS Hispeed *Fyra* trains, the ride takes 40 minutes, and on ordinary InterCity trains 70 minutes. The round-trip fare is 27€. Once in Rotterdam, you can use the trams and the Metro with the same OV-chipkaart public transportation card you used in Amsterdam. Taxis are plentiful, too.

For information, visit **ROTTERDAM.INFO,** Coolsingel 195–197, 3012 AG Rotterdam (☎ **0900/403-4065;** www.vvvrotterdam.nl; Metro: Beurs), close to the corner of Westblaak. The office is open Monday to Friday from 10am to 7pm, Saturday from 9:30am to 6pm, and Sunday from 10am to 5pm.

The **Hague & Scheveningen**

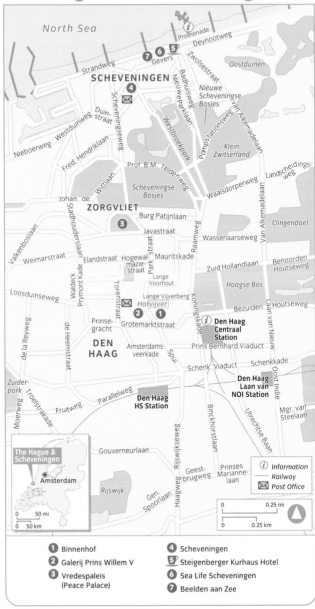

1 Binnenhof

2 Galerij Prins Willem V

3 Vredespaleis
   (Peace Palace)

4 Scheveningen

5 Steigenberger Kurhaus Hotel

6 Sea Life Scheveningen

7 Beelden aan Zee

The capital of the Netherlands is stately and grand, and its neighboring seacoast resort Scheveningen provides a lovely escape. A day here affords you a fantastic opportunity to visit the Peace Palace, home to the International Court of Justice, and the Binnenhof, the grand seat of the Dutch Parliament. The Hague (known in Dutch as Den Haag, or more formally as 's-Gravenhage) is only an hour away from Amsterdam, but you may consider spending a night here to have some beach time. START: **A 10-minute tram ride from Den Haag Centraal Station brings you to the center city at Buitenhof, the Outer Court of Holland's Parliament.**

❶ ★★★ Binnenhof (Inner Court).

At this venerable complex of Parliament buildings, join a tour to visit the lofty, medieval Ridderzaal (Hall of the Knights), where the queen delivers a speech from the throne each year to open the new legislative session. Depending on the volume and urgency of government business, you may be able to tour one or the other of the two chambers of the Staaten-Generaal (States General), the Dutch Parliament. ⏱ *2 hr. Binnenhof 8A.* ☎ *070/364-6144. www.binnenhofbezoek.nl. Admission 6€ or 4€ adults (varies with the tour being offered). Guided tours (the only way you can visit) are hourly Mon–Sat 10am–4pm; call ahead to reserve a tour and to confirm availability (occasionally tours are canceled). Tram: 10, 16, or 17 to Buitenhof.*

❷ ★ Galerij Prins Willem V.

The country's first art gallery opened in 1774 to display the private collection of Prince of Orange Willem V. Today it is owned by the Mauritshuis (see "Masters on the Move," below). Paintings by Dutch Old Masters from the "Golden Age" period are displayed in a cluttered style. There are few internationally known works, but all the paintings are interesting and have a cumulative impact. Look out for Jan Steen's shiver-inducing *The Toothpuller* (1651). ⏱ *2 hr. Buitenhof 33 (across the street from the Binnenhof).* ☎ *070/302-3435. www.mauritshuis. nl. Admission 5€ adults, 2.50€ kids 6–12. Tues–Sun noon–5pm. Closed Jan 1, Dec 25. Tram: 10, 16, or 17 to Buitenhof.*

Binnenhof.

A display from the Galerij Prins Willem V.

❸ ★ Vredespaleis (Peace Palace). You'll have to call ahead for a tour reservation, but this could easily be the highlight of your trip to The Hague. Andrew Carnegie donated over a million dollars to the construction of this magnificent mock-Gothic Palace, home to the International Court of Justice and the Permanent Court of Arbitration. The building was designed by French architect Louis Cordonnier and completed in 1913. On the tour, you'll be able to visit most of the rooms and marvel at gifts given by each of the participating countries: crystal chandeliers (each weighing 1,750kg/3,858 lb.) from Delft, made with real rubies and emeralds; incredible mosaic floors from France; 140 kinds of marble from Italy; a huge Turkish carpet woven in 1926 in Izmir; and an immense 3,500-kilograms (7,716-lb.) vase from Czar Nicolas of Russia. If the courts are not in session, your guide will take you inside the International Court of Justice, which handles all of the United Nations' judicial cases. ⏱ *2 hr. Carnegieplein 2.* ☎ *070/302-4137. www.vredespaleis. nl. Admission 5€ adults, 3€ kids 6–12. Tours May–Sept Mon–Fri 10 and 11am & 2, 3, and 4pm; Oct–Apr Mon–Fri 10 and 11am & 2 and 3pm. Reservations required; it's not possible to visit the palace on your own. Tram: 1 or 10 to Vredespaleis.*

❹ ★★ Scheveningen. This relaxed, beachside town is only a 15-minute tram ride from the center of The Hague. It has a wide, sandy beach and a charming pier affording great views of the North Sea. Pleasant cafes line the waterfront boardwalk, and on summer weekends sun worshipers fill the beach. Towering over both the town and the beach is the majestic Steigenberger Kurhaus Hotel (see below), which is a good place for a drink or a meal with fine views of the water. If you're in the mood for some outdoor activity, you can also take a long walk over the rolling sand dunes that dot the coast for miles. *Tram: 1, 9, or 11 to*

The wide, sandy beach at Scheveningen.

Masters on the Move

The Mauritshuis, a palace that houses the Koninklijk Kabinet van Schilderijen (Royal Cabinet of Paintings), a collection of Dutch Old Masters, is slated to close in April 2012 for 2 years of reconstruction and refurbishment. During this time, important works—including Vermeer's famous *View of Delft* (1661) and *Girl with a Pearl Earring* (ca. 1665)—will be displayed at other galleries and museums around The Hague, primarily in the Gemeentemuseum Den Haag (www.gemeentemuseum.nl). To keep abreast of progress, visit www.mauritshuis.nl.

the beach; 10, 11, or 17 to the fishing harbor. The ride on tram 9 from Scheveningen back to Den Haag Centraal Station takes 20 min.

5 ★★★ **Steigenberger Kurhaus Hotel.** While in Scheveningen, stop for a drink or a snack in the conservatory and terrace at the Steigenberger Kurhaus Hotel, which has views of the North Sea. If you're here on a cold afternoon, consider having the traditional English-style "high tea" in the ultragracious Kurzaal restaurant. *Gevers Deynootplein 30.* ☎ *070/416-2636. www.kurhaus.nl. Serre & Terras daily 10am–10pm; high tea daily 2:30–4:30pm. $$.*

6 kids **Sea Life Scheveningen.** This large aquarium has a walk-through underwater tunnel that lets you observe the denizens of the deep, including sharks swimming around above your head. ⏱ *1 hr. Strandweg (also known as the Boulevard) 13.* ☎ *070/354-2100. www. visitsealife.com. Admission 15€ adults, 13€ seniors & people with disabilities, 10€ kids 3–11 (purchase online and save 3€ on each ticket). Sept–June daily 10am–6pm; July–Aug daily 10am–8pm. Tram: 1 to Scheveningseslag.*

7 ★ **Beelden aan Zee.** A highlight of your trip to Scheveningen may be this fine sculpture museum

Kids will love seeing the sea creatures at Sea Life Scheveningen.

The outdoor sculpture garden at Beelden aan Zee.

built into the sand dunes just steps from the busy boardwalk. Take some time to admire the construction and the use of natural light that spills into the main hall. Terraces overlooking the sea are strewn with sculptures and the indoor galleries look out onto the sand dunes and the sea beyond. Most of the sculptures are of human figures, and the sculptors hail from all over the world. One of my favorites is the marble *Venus* (1984) by Dutch sculptor Jan Meefout. Outside the museum, on the boardwalk, you'll find the Fairy Figures by the Sea, a permanent installation that's free of charge. The huge, cartoon-like sculptures are all by New Yorker Tom Otterness. Leave some time to stroll around after you visit, admiring the sculptures from the pier and the beach. ⏱ *1½ hr. Hartevelstraat 1 (off Gevers Deynootweg).* ☎ *070/358-5857. www.beeldenaanzee.nl. Admission 9.50€ adults, 4.75€ kids 13–18. Tues–Sun 11am–5pm. Tram: 1 to Scheveningseslag.* ●

The Hague Basics

The Hague is about an hour from Amsterdam's Centraal Station, and there are up to six trains an hour. A round-trip ticket is 21€. The Hague has two main rail stations, Den Haag Centraal Station and Den Haag HS; most sights are closer to Centraal Station, but some trains stop only at HS. Once you arrive at Den Haag Centraal Station, you'll find trams adjacent to the station. To get around, you can use an OV-chipkaart transit card or an HTM dagkaart (day ticket; 6.80€), which affords you unlimited use of public transportation in The Hague and Scheveningen.

For information, **VVV Den Haag,** Hofweg 1, 2511 AA Den Haag (☎ **070/361-8860;** www.denhaag.nl), is close to the Binnenhof (Parliament). The office is open Monday from noon to 6pm, Tuesday to Friday from 9:30am to 6pm, Saturday from 9:30am to 5pm, and Sunday from 11am to 5pm.

The
Savvy Traveler

Before You Go

Government Tourist Offices

For the U.S. & Canada: Netherlands Board of Tourism & Conventions (NBTC), 215 Park Avenue South, Ste. 2005, New York, NY 10003 (☎ 212/370-7360; fax 212/370-9507; www.holland.com). **For the U.K. & Ireland:** No walk-in service. NBTC, PO Box 30783, London WC2B 6DH (☎ 020/7539-7950; fax 020/7539-7953; www.holland.com/uk). **In Holland:** No walk-in service. NBTC, Postbus 458, 2260 MG Leidschendam (☎ 31-70/370-5705; fax 31-70/3370-5368; www.nbtc.nl).

The Best Times to Go

"In season" in Amsterdam means from mid-April to mid-October. The peak of the tourist season is July and August, when the weather is at its finest. Weather, however, is never really extreme at any time of year, and if you're one of the growing numbers who favor shoulder- or off-season travel, you'll find the city every bit as attractive. Not only are airlines, hotels, and restaurants cheaper and less crowded during the off season (with more relaxed and personalized service), but there are also some very appealing events going on. You may want to go when the bulb fields near Amsterdam are bursting with color from April to mid-May, one of the best times to visit Holland.

Festivals & Special Events

SPRING. Late March to mid-May, catch the **Opening of Keukenhof Gardens,** Lisse. The greatest flower show on earth blooms with a spectacular display of tulips, narcissi, daffodils, hyacinths, bluebells, crocuses, lilies, amaryllis, and many other flowers at this 32-hectare (79-acre) garden in the heart of the bulb country. There's said to be nearly eight million flowers, but who's counting? Contact **Keukenhof** (☎ 0252/465-555; www.keukenhof.nl).

During **Museum Weekend** (the second weekend in Apr), most museums in Amsterdam and many throughout the Netherlands offer free or reduced admission and have special exhibits. Contact **Museum-vereniging/Museumweekend** (☎ 020/551-2900; www.museumweekend.nl).

On April 30, Amsterdam celebrates **Koninginnedag (Queen's Day)** with a gigantic dawn-to-dawn street carnival. The center city gets so jampacked with people that it's virtually impossible to move. A city-wide street market features masses of stalls. Orange ribbons, orange hair, and orange-painted faces are everywhere, as are Dutch flags. Street music and theater combine with lots of drinking during this good-natured if boisterous affair. *Tip:* Wear something orange, even if it's only an orange cap or an orange ribbon in your hair. Contact **Amsterdam Tourist Information** (☎ 020/201-8800; www.iamsterdam.com) for more information.

The second Saturday in May is **National Windmill Day** throughout Holland. Around two-thirds of the country's almost 1,000 remaining working windmills spin their sails and are open to the public; among them are Amsterdam's eight. Contact **De Hollandsche Molen** (☎ 020/623-8703; www.molens.nl).

SUMMER. From June through August, catch a performance at the

Previous page: Amsterdam's bustling Centraal Station.

Vondelpark Open-Air Theater. Everything goes here: theater, all kinds of music (including full-scale classical concerts by the famed Royal Concertgebouw Orchestra), dance, and even operettas. Contact **Vondelpark Openluchttheater** (☎ 020/428-3360; www.open luchttheater.nl).

The **Amsterdam Roots Festival,** which runs for 5 days toward the end of June at various venues around town, features world music and dance, along with workshops, films, and exhibits. One part is **Roots Open Air,** a multicultural feast of song and dance held at Oosterpark in Amsterdam-Oost (East). Contact **Amsterdam Roots Festival** (☎ 020/531-8181; www. amsterdamroots.nl).

In the third week of June, **Open Garden Days** is your chance to find out what the fancy gardens behind the gables of some of the city's houses-turned-museums look like. A number of the best gardens are open to the public for 3 days. Contact **Grachten Musea** (☎ 020/320-3660; www.grachtenmusea.nl) for more information.

One of the world's leading gatherings of top international jazz and blues musicians, the **North Sea Jazz Festival** unfolds over 3 concert-packed mid-July days at Rotterdam's giant Ahoy venue. Last-minute tickets are scarce, so book as far ahead as possible. Contact **North Sea Jazz Festival** (☎ 0900/300-1250 in Holland; 31-10/592-7925 from outside Holland; www.northseajazz.com).

Europe's most gay-friendly city hosts the **Amsterdam Gay Pride** event over 3 days in early August. A crowd of 150,000 people turns out to watch the highlight Canal Parade, in which some 100 outrageously decorated boats cruise the canals. In addition, there are street discos, open-air theater performances, a sports program, and a film festival. Go to the website of **Amsterdam Gay Pride** (www.amsterdam gaypride.nl) for more information.

The 10-day classical music **Grachtenfestival (Canals Festival)** plays in mid-August at various intimate and elegant venues along the canals and at the Muziekgebouw aan 't IJ. Closing out the festival is the exuberant Prinsengracht Concert, which is presented on a pontoon in front of the Hotel Pulitzer (p 132). Contact **Stichting Grachtenfestival** (☎ 020/421-4542; www.grachtenfestival.nl) for more information.

Amsterdam previews its cultural season with the **Uitmarkt,** usually the last weekend in August. A 3-day "open information market" runs alongside free performances of music, opera, dance, theater, and cabaret at theaters, concert halls, and impromptu outdoor venues around the city. Go to the website of **Uitmarkt** (www.amsterdams uitburo.nl/uitmarkt) for more information.

FALL. During **Open Monumentendag,** on the second Saturday in September, you have a chance to see historical buildings and monuments that are usually not open to the public—and to get in free as well. Contact **Stichting Open Monumentendag** (☎ 020/422-2118; www.openmonumentendag.nl) for more information.

On the third Sunday in September, starting at noon, participants in the popular **Dam tot Damloop (Dam to Dam Run),** start at the Dam in the center of Amsterdam, head out of town through the IJ Tunnel to the center of Zaandam, and return to the Dam, for a distance of 16km (10 miles). Contact **Dam tot Damloop** (☎ 072/533-8136; www.damloop.nl) for more information.

On the third Tuesday in September, Queen Beatrix rides in a splendid gold coach to the Ridderzaal (Hall of the Knights) in The Hague for the **State Opening of Parliament,** which opens the legislative session. Contact **VVV Den Haag** (☎ 0900/340-3505, or 31-70/361-8860 from outside the Netherlands; www.denhaag.nl) for more information.

WINTER. **Sinterklaas,** Holland's equivalent of Santa Claus (St. Nicholas) launches the Christmas season on the third Saturday of November, when he arrives in the city by boat at the Centraal Station pier. Accompanied by black-painted assistants called *Zwarte Piet* (Black Peter) who hand out candy to kids along the way, he goes in stately procession through Amsterdam before being given the keys to the city by the mayor at the Dam. Contact **Amsterdam Tourist Information** (☎ 020/201-8800; www.iamsterdam.com) for more information.

The city's **New Year's** celebrations take place throughout the center city on the night of December 31 to January 1, but mostly at the Dam and Nieuwmarkt. Things can get wild and not always so wonderful. Many of Amsterdam's youthful spirits celebrate the new year with firecrackers, which they throw at the feet of passersby. This keeps hospital emergency departments busy.

More than 300 indie films are screened at theaters around town during the **International Film Festival Rotterdam,** from late January to early February. Contact (☎ 010/890-9090; www.filmfestival rotterdam.com) for more information.

The Weather

Summers are warm and pleasant, with only a few oppressively hot days. However, air-conditioned hotels are rare, so those few days can be quite uncomfortable. Rain is common throughout the year, especially in winter.

Useful Websites

- **www.visitholland.com** offers comprehensive information, covering hotels, sightseeing, and notices of special events.

- **www.amsterdamhotspots.nl** lists the latest places to see and be seen in the city.

- **www.museum.nl** is loaded with information about the city's museums—more than 40 of them.

- **www.iamsterdam.com**, the city tourist office's website, is a virtually inexhaustible resource.

Cellphones (Mobile Phones)

If your phone has GSM (Global System for Mobiles) capability and you have a world-compatible phone, you should be able to make and receive calls in Holland. Only certain phones have this capability, though, and you should check with your service operator first. Call charges can be high. Alternatively, you can rent a phone through **Cellhire** (www.cellhire.com; www.cellhire.co.uk; www.cellhire.com.au). After a simple online registration, they will ship a phone (usually with a U.K. number) to your home or office. Usage charges can be astronomical, so read the fine print.

U.K. mobiles work in Holland; call your service provider before departing your home country to ensure that the international call bar has been switched off and to check call charges, which can be extremely high. Also remember that you are charged for calls you *receive* on a U.K. mobile used abroad.

Car Rentals

There's very little need to rent a car in Amsterdam, but if you're determined to do so, it's usually cheapest to book a car online before you leave home.

AMSTERDAM'S AVERAGE MONTHLY TEMPERATURES

	JAN	FEB	MAR	APR	MAY	JUNE	JULY	AUG	SEPT	OCT	NOV	DEC
Temp. (°F)	38	37	43	47	54	59	62	62	58	51	44	40
Temp. (°C)	3	3	6	8	12	15	17	17	14	11	7	4

Try **Hertz** (www.hertz.com), **Avis** (www.avis.com), **Budget** (www.budget.com), or **Europcar** (www.europcar.com). You should also consider **AutoEurope** (www.autoeurope.com), which sends you a pre-paid voucher, locking in the exchange rate.

Getting **There**

By Plane
Arriving: Amsterdam Airport Schiphol (☎ 0900/0141 for general and flight information, 31-20/794-0800 from outside Holland; www.schiphol.nl; airport code AMS), 13km (8 miles) southwest of the city center, is the main airport in the Netherlands, handling just about all of the country's international arrivals and departures. Frequent travelers regularly vote Schiphol (pronounced *Skhip*-ol), one of the world's favorite airports for its ease of use and its massive, duty-free shopping center.

After you deplane at one of the three terminals (all close together and numbered 1, 2, and 3), moving walkways take you to the Arrivals Hall, where you pass through Passport Control, Customs, and Baggage Reclaim. Conveniences like free luggage carts (baggage trolleys), currency exchange, ATMs, restaurants, bars, shops, baby rooms, restrooms, and showers are available. Beyond these is Schiphol Plaza, which combines rail station access, the Airport Hotel, a mall (sporting that most essential Dutch service—a flower store), bars and restaurants, restrooms, baggage lockers, airport and tourist information desks, car-rental and hotel-reservation desks, and more, all in a single location. Bus and shuttle stops and a taxi stand are just outside.

For tourist information and to make hotel reservations, go to the **Holland Tourist Information** desk in Schiphol Plaza (☎ 0900/400-4040); it is open daily from 7am to 10pm.

Getting into town: Netherlands Railways (NS) **trains** (☎ 0900/9292; www.ns.nl) depart from Schiphol Station to Amsterdam Centraal Station, downstairs from Schiphol Plaza; trains stop at De Lelylaan and De Vlugtlaan stations in west Amsterdam on the way. Frequency ranges from six trains an hour at peak times to one an hour at night. The fare is 3.70€ one-way; the ride takes 15 to 20 minutes.

An alternative rail route serves both Amsterdam Zuid station and Amsterdam RAI station (beside the RAI Convention Center). If you're staying at a hotel near Leidseplein, Rembrandtplein, in the Museum District, or in Amsterdam South, this route may be a better bet for you than Centraal Station. The fare is 2.50€ one-way; the ride takes around 15 minutes. From Zuid, take tram no. 5 for Leidseplein and the Museum District; from Amsterdam RAI, take tram no. 4 for Rembrandtplein.

The **Connexxion Schiphol Hotel Shuttle** (☎ 038/339-4741; www.schipholhotelshuttle.nl) runs between the airport and Amsterdam, serving around 100 hotels either directly or because they are close to the direct stops. The fare is 16€ one-way and 25€ round-trip; kids 4–14 pay half the adult fare. No reservations are needed and buses depart from in front of Schiphol Plaza every 10 to 30 minutes daily from 6am to 9pm. The bus ride takes anywhere from 40 minutes to 1½ hours.

The **Connexxion bus no. 197** departs every 15 minutes or so from in front of Schiphol Plaza for Amsterdam's downtown Marnixstraat bus station (the line number is N97 at night, and the frequency is hourly). The fare is 4€. The bus ride takes about 40 minutes.

You'll find **taxis** waiting at the stand of **SchipholTaxi** (☎ 0900/900-6666; www.schipholtaxi.nl) in front of Schiphol Plaza. Taxis from the airport are metered. Expect to pay 40€ to 50€ to the center of Amsterdam; the ride takes 35 to 45 minutes. A service charge is already included in the fare.

By Boat from Britain

DFDS Seaways (☎ 0871/522-9955 in Britain, 0255/546-666 in Holland; www.dfdsseaways.co.uk) has daily car-ferry service between Newcastle in northeast England and IJmuiden on the North Sea coast west of Amsterdam. The overnight travel time is 15½ hours. From IJmuiden, you can go by special bus to Amsterdam Centraal Station.

P&O Ferries (☎ 08716/642121 in Britain, 020/200-8333 in Holland; www.poferries.com) has daily car-ferry service between Hull in northeast England and Rotterdam (Europoort). The overnight travel time is 10–11 hours. Ferry-company buses shuttle passengers between the Rotterdam Europoort terminal

and Rotterdam Centraal Station, from where there are frequent trains to Amsterdam.

Stena Line (☎ 08447/707070 in Britain, 0900/8123 in Holland, or 31-174/315-811 from outside Holland; www.stenaline.co.uk) has twice-daily car-ferry service between Harwich in southeast England and Hoek van Holland (Hook of Holland) near Rotterdam. The travel time is 6 hours, 45 minutes for the daytime crossing, and 7½ hours for the overnight. Frequent trains depart from Hoek van Holland to Amsterdam.

By Cruise Ship

Cruise-ship passengers arrive in Amsterdam at the **Passenger Terminal Amsterdam,** Piet Heinkade 27 (☎ 020/509-1000; www.pt amsterdam.nl; tram 25 or 26), on the IJ waterway within easy walking distance of Centraal Station.

By Train

Rail service to Amsterdam from other cities in the Netherlands and elsewhere in Europe is frequent and fast. International trains arrive at Centraal Station from Brussels, Paris, Berlin, Cologne, and other German cities, and from more cities in Austria, Switzerland, Italy, and eastern Europe. **Nederlandse Spoorwegen** (Netherlands Railways; www.ns.nl) trains arrive in Amsterdam from towns and cities all over Holland. Service is frequent to many places around the country and trains are modern, clean, and punctual. Schedule and fare information on travel by train is available by calling ☎ 0900/9292 for national service, and 0900/9296 for international; or by visiting www.ns.nl.

The burgundy-colored **Thalys** (www.thalys.com) high-speed train, with a top speed of 300kmph (186 mph), connects Paris, Brussels, Amsterdam, and (via Brussels)

Cologne. Travel time from Paris to Amsterdam is 4 hours, 10 minutes, and from Brussels 1 hour, 45 minutes. For Thalys information and reservations, call ☎ **3635** in France; ☎ **070/797-979** in Belgium; ☎ **11861** in Germany; and ☎ **0900/9296** in Holland. Tickets are also available from many railway stations and travel agents.

On the **Eurostar** (www.eurostar.com) high-speed train (top speed 300kmph/186 mph), the travel time between London St. Pancras Station and Brussels's Bruxelles-Midi Station (the closest connecting point for Amsterdam) is around 2 hours. Departures from London to Brussels are approximately every 2 hours at peak times. For Eurostar reservations, call ☎ **08432/186186** in Britain.

Arriving at Centraal Station: Regardless of where they originate, most visitors traveling to Amsterdam by train find themselves deposited at Amsterdam's Centraal Station, built from 1884 to 1889 on an artificial island in the IJ channel. The building, an ornate architectural wonder on its own, is the focus of much activity. It's at the hub of the city's concentric rings of canals and connecting main streets, and is the originating point for most of the city's trams, Metro trains, and buses.

You'll find an office of Amsterdam Tourist Information right in front of the station on Stationsplein; the office has hotel-reservation desks. Other station facilities include a GWK Travelex currency-exchange office, ATMs, a train info center, luggage lockers, restaurants and snack bars, newsstands, and specialty stores.

Warning: Centraal Station is home to a pickpocket convention that's in full swing at all times. Messages broadcast in multiple languages warn people to be on their guard, but the artful dodgers still seem to do good business. Avoid becoming one of their victims by keeping your money and other valuables under wraps, especially among crowds.

An array of tram stops are on either side of the main station exit— virtually all of Amsterdam's hotels are within a 15-minute tram ride from Centraal Station. The Metro station is downstairs, just outside the main exit. City bus stops are to the left of the main exit, and the taxi stands are to the right. At the public transportation GVB Tickets & Info office on Stationsplein, you can buy cards for trams, Metro trains, and buses (see "Getting Around," below, for more information). The station is also a departure point for passenger ferries across the IJ waterway, water taxis, canal-boat tours, the Museum Line boats, and the Canal Bus.

By Bus

International coaches—and in particular those of Eurolines—arrive at the bus terminal opposite the Amstel rail station (Metro: Amstel) in the south of the city. Eurolines operates coach service between London Victoria Bus Station and Amstel Station (via ferry), with up to five departures daily in the summer. Travel time is just over 12 hours. For reservations, contact **Eurolines** (☎ 08717/818181 in Britain or 020/560-8788 in Holland; www.eurolines.com). From here, you can go by train or Metro train to Centraal Station, or by tram no. 12 to the Museumplein area and to connecting points for trams to the center city. For the Leidseplein area, take the Metro toward Centraal Station, get out at Weesperplein, and go aboveground to take tram 7 or 10.

By Car

A network of major international highways crisscrosses Holland. European expressways E19, E35, E231, and E22 converge on Amsterdam from France and Belgium to the south and from Germany to the north and east. These roads also have Dutch designations; as you approach the city they are, respectively: A4, A2, A1, and A7. Amsterdam's ring road is A10. Distances between destinations are relatively short. Traffic is invariably heavy, but road conditions are otherwise excellent, service stations are plentiful, and highways are plainly signposted.

Getting **Around**

By Public Transportation
Most public transportation in the Netherlands uses an electronic stored-value card called the **OV-chipkaart.** There are three main types of OV-chipkaart: "personal" cards that can be used only by their pictured owner; "anonymous" cards that can be used by anyone; and "throwaway" cards. The personal and anonymous cards, both valid for 5 years, cost 7.50€ and can be loaded and reloaded with up to 30€. Throwaway cards, which are likely to be the card of choice for short-term visitors, cost 2.50€ for one ride and 4.80€ for two rides. Reduced-rate cards are available for seniors and children. Electronic readers on Metro and train station platforms and onboard trams and buses deduct the correct fare; just hold your card up against the reader at both the start and the end of the ride.
Remember: These cards are valid not just in Amsterdam, but also everywhere in Holland, no matter where you buy them or use them.

A better bet for short-term visitors who plan to use public transportation a lot is a 1-day or a multiday card: 24 hours (7.50€), 48 hours (12€), 72 hours (15€), 96 hours (18€), 120 hours (23€), 144 hours (26€), 168 hours (29€).

The central information and ticket sales point for GVB Amsterdam, the city's public transportation company, is **GVB Tickets & Info,** Stationsplein (☎ 0900/9292 for timetable and fare information,

0900/8011 for other customer services; www.gvb.nl), in front of Centraal Station, open Monday to Friday from 7am to 9pm, Saturday and Sunday from 8am to 9pm. In addition, cards are available from GVB and Netherlands Railways ticket booths in Metro and train stations, ticket machines (automats) at Metro and train stations, and ticket machines onboard some trams.

By Tram: Half the fun of Amsterdam is walking along the canals. The other half is riding the blue-and-light-gray trams that roll through most major streets. There are 16 tram routes, 10 of which (lines 1, 2, 4, 5, 9, 13, 16, 17, 24, and 26) begin and end at Centraal Station; another (line 25) passes through. So you know you can always get back to that central point if you get lost and have to start over. The city's other tram lines are 3, 7, 10, 12, and 14. ***Note:*** Due to renovation work, line 4 won't ply its usual route on the Muntplein-Rembrandtplein-Utrechtsestraat-Frederiksplein stretch (see the Amsterdam Transit map on the front cover fold-out map) until late 2012. Until then, the line follows an alternative route: Muntplein-Weteringcircuit-Frederiksplein.

Most trams have just one available access door that opens automatically; you board toward the rear (in the case of the oldest trams, at the rear) following arrowed indicators that point the way to the door. To board a tram that has no such arrowed indicators, push the button on the outside of the car beside any door. To get off, you may need to push a button with an "open-door" graphic or the words *Deur Open*. Tram doors close automatically, and they do it quite quickly, so don't hang around.

By Bus: An extensive bus network complements the trams. Many bus routes begin and end at €entraal Station. It's generally faster to go by tram if you have the option, but some points in the city are served only by bus.

By Metro: The Metro can't compare to the labyrinthine systems of Paris, London, and New York, but Amsterdam does have its own Metro, with four lines—50, 51, 53, and 54—that run partly overground and bring people in from the suburbs and home again. You may want to take them simply as a sightseeing excursion, though to be frank, few of the sights on the lines are worth going out of your way for. From Centraal Station, you can use Metro trains to reach both Nieuwmarkt and Waterlooplein in the central zone.

A new Metro line, the Noord/Zuidlijn, is currently under construction to link Amsterdam-Noord (North), under the IJ waterway, with the center city and then Amsterdam Zuid station. It's due to be completed in 2017.

By Ferry: Free ferries for passengers and two-wheel transportation connect the center city with Amsterdam-Noord (North), across the IJ waterway. The short crossings are free, which makes them ideal micro-cruises for the cash strapped, and they afford fine views of the harbor. Ferries depart from Waterplein West, a dock on De Ruijterkade behind Centraal Station. One route goes to Buiksloterweg on the north shore, with ferries every 6 to 12 minutes round-the-clock. A second route goes to IJplein, a more easterly point on the north shore, with

ferries every 8 to 15 minutes from 6:30am to around midnight. A third ferry goes west to NDSM-Werf, a 14-minute trip that affords a decent view of the harbor.

By Water Bus: Two different companies operate water buses (rarely, if ever, used by locals) that bring you to, or close to, many of the city's museums, attractions, and shopping and entertainment districts. **Canal Bus** (☎ 0900/333-4442; www.canal.nl) has four routes—Green, Red, Blue, and Orange—with stops that include Centraal Station, Westermarkt, Leidseplein, Rijksmuseum (with an extension to the RAI Convention Center when big shows are on there), and Waterlooplein. Hours of operation are daily from 10am to 6:30pm, with two buses an hour at peak times. A day pass that affords discounted admission to some museums and attractions, is 20€ for adults, and 10€ for kids ages 4 to 12.

The **Museum Line** (☎ 020/530-1090; www.lovers.nl) boats transport weary visitors on their pilgrimages from museum to museum and have the added benefit of providing some of the features of a canal-boat cruise. Boats depart from the Rederij Lovers dock in front of Centraal Station daily from 10am to 5:30pm, every 30 minutes in summer, and every 45 minutes in winter. They stop at key spots around town, providing access to museums and other sights. These include the Rijksmuseum, Van Gogh Museum, Stedelijk Museum, Anne Frankhuis, Museum Het Rembrandthuis, and Jewish Historical Museum. A ticket is 15€ for adults, and 7.50€ for kids ages 4 to 12. Tickets include discounted admission to some museums and attractions.

By Taxi

It used to be that you couldn't simply hail a cab from the street in

Amsterdam, but nowadays they often stop if you do. Otherwise, find one of the taxi stands sprinkled around the city, generally near the luxury hotels, at major squares such as the Dam, Spui, Rembrandtplein, Westermarkt, and Leidseplein, and of course at Centraal Station. Taxis have rooftop signs and blue license tags, and are metered.

For a generally reliable service, call **Taxi Centrale Amsterdam** (TCA; ☎ 020/777-7777). TCA's fares begin at 7.50€ when the meter starts and run up at 2.20€ a kilometer, and after 25km (16 miles), 1.75€ a kilometer. The fare includes a tip, but you may round up or give something for an extra service, like help with your luggage, or for a helpful discourse.

By Water Taxi

Since you're in the city of canals, you might like to splurge on a water taxi. These launches do more or less the same thing as landlubber taxis, except that they do it on the canals and the Amstel River and in the harbor. You can move faster than on land and you get your very own canal cruise. To order one, call **VIP Water-taxi** (☎ 020/535-6363; www.water-taxi.nl), or pick one up from the dock outside Centraal Station, close to the VVV office. For up to eight people, the fare is 20€ for 30 minutes in the city center, and 50€ for 30 minutes outside the city center.

By Bike

Instead of renting a car, follow the Dutch example and ride a bicycle. Sunday, when the city is quiet, is a particularly good day to pedal through Vondelpark and along off-the-beaten-path canals, or to practice riding on cobblestones and in bike lanes, crossing bridges, and dodging trams before venturing forth into the fray of an Amsterdam rush hour. There are half a million

bikes in the city, so you'll have plenty of company.

Navigating the city on two wheels is mostly safe—or at any rate not as suicidal as it looks—thanks to a vast network of dedicated bike lanes. Bikes even have their own traffic lights. Amsterdam's battle-scarred bike-borne veterans make it almost a point of principle to ignore every safety rule ever written. Though they mostly live to tell the tale, don't think the same will necessarily apply to you.

Bike-rental rates start at 12€ a day or 50€ a week; a deposit is required. **Mike's Bike Tours,** Kerk-straat 134 (☎ 020/622-7970; www.mikesbiketoursamsterdam.com; tram 1, 2, or 5), is a good bet for a rental. So is **MacBike** (☎ 020/620-0985; www.macbike.nl), which rents a range of bikes, including tandems and six-speed touring bikes, and has rental outlets at Stationsplein 5 (Metro: Centraal Station); Water-looplein 199 (tram 9 or 14); Marnix-straat 220 (tram 10, 13, 14, or 17); and Weteringschans 2 (tram 1, 2, 5, 7, or 10).

Warning: Always lock both your bike frame and one of the wheels to something solid and fixed, because theft is common.

By Car

Driving in Amsterdam is not recommended. Parking is difficult, traffic is dense, and networks of one-way streets make navigation, even with the best of maps, a problem. You would be much better advised to make use of the city's extensive public transportation or to take cabs.

By Foot

The best way to take in the city is to walk, and the center city is pedestrian-friendly. Carry a good map with you, and watch out for those ubiquitous speeding bikes and speeding trams.

Fast **Facts**

ATM/CASHPOINTS The easiest and best way to get cash abroad is through an ATM—the **Cirrus** and **Plus** networks span the globe. Most banks charge a fee for international withdrawals—check with your bank before you leave home, and find out your daily limit. There are many ATMs in Amsterdam, and in the center of town you'll be virtually tripping over the things. Many of them are open 24/7, though you'll want to be a little bit cautious about withdrawing cash in quiet areas after dark.

BABYSITTERS Many mid- and upper-range Amsterdam hotels can arrange babysitting services. A reliable local organization is **Oppascentrale Kriterion** (☎ 020/624-5848; www.oppascentralekriterion.nl), which has vetted babysitters over 18. Its rates are 7€ an hour for a minimum of 3 hours, plus a 3€ administration charge per booking; a possible deal-breaker is the 25€ registration fee.

BANKS Among the leading Dutch banks, ABN AMRO (www.abnamro.nl), ING (www.ing.com), Rabobank (www.rabobank.nl), and SNS (www.snsbank.nl) all have multiple branches around Amsterdam. Most banks are open Monday to Friday from 9am to 4, 5, or 6pm (some stay open Thurs until 7pm). A few are open on Saturday morning. Some shops and most hotels will cash traveler's checks but not at the advantageous rate most banks and foreign exchanges will give you.

BIKE RENTALS See "By Bike," under "Getting Around," earlier in this chapter.

BUSINESS HOURS Shops tend to be open from 9:30am to 6pm. Some stay open until 8 or 9pm. Most museums close 1 day a week (often Mon), but may be open some holidays, except Koninginnedag (Queen's Day), Christmas, and New Year's Day.

CONSULATES & EMBASSIES **U.K. Consulate:** Koningslaan 44 (☎ 020/676-4343; www.britain.nl; tram 2). **U.S. Consulate:** Museumplein 19 (☎ 020/575-5330; http://amsterdam.usconsulate.gov; tram 3, 5, 12, or 16).

Embassies are in The Hague (Den Haag): **Australian Embassy,** Carnegielaan 4 (☎ 070/310-8200; www.netherlands.embassy.gov.au). **Canadian Embassy,** Sophialaan 7 (☎ 070/311-1600; www.canada.nl). **Irish Embassy,** Scheveningseweg 112 (☎ 070/363-0993; www.irish embassy.nl). **New Zealand Embassy,** Eisenhowerlaan 77N (☎ 070/346-9324; www.nz embassy.com/netherlands).

U.K. Embassy, Lange Voorhout 10 (☎ 070/427-0427; www.britain.nl). **U.S. Embassy,** Lange Voorhout 102 (☎ 070/310-2209; http://the hague.usembassy.gov).

CREDIT CARDS In Holland, you'll rarely if ever come across a business that uses the old swipe system for authorizing credit card payments. Instead, payments will either be authorized by a chip system in the card and the cardholder's signature, or by chip-and-PIN, with a four-digit personal identification number replacing the signature. You can withdraw cash advances from your credit cards at banks or ATMs provided you know your PIN. Keep in mind that when you use your credit card abroad, most banks assess a 2% fee above the 1% fee charged by Visa, MasterCard, and American Express. You also pay interest from the day of your withdrawal, even if you pay your monthly bill on time.

CURRENCY EXCHANGE Cash your traveler's checks at banks or

foreign-exchange offices, not at shops or hotels. Most post offices also change traveler's checks or convert money. Currency exchanges are found at Amsterdam's Schiphol Airport and Centraal Station.

CUSTOMS   Travelers arriving from a **non–European Union country** can bring in, duty-free, 200 cigarettes (or 250g of tobacco), or 100 cigarillos (or 50 cigars); 1 liter of alcohol over 22 proof, or 2 liters under 22 proof, 4 liters of wine, and 16 liters of beer; and 50ml of perfume or 0.25 liters of eau de toilette. Travelers arriving from an **E.U. country** can bring any amount of goods into the Netherlands, so long as they are intended for personal use and not for resale; there are generous guideline limits, beyond which the goods may be deemed to be for resale.

DENTISTS   See "Emergencies," below.

DOCTORS   See "Emergencies," below.

DRUGSTORES   In the Netherlands, a pharmacy is called an *apotheek* and sells both prescription and nonprescription medicines. Regular open hours are Monday to Saturday from 9am to 6pm. A centrally located pharmacy is **Dam Apotheek,** Damstraat 2 (☎ 020/624-4331; www. dam-apotheek.nl; tram 4, 9, 14, 16, 24, or 25), close to the Nationaal Monument on the Dam. Pharmacies post details of nearby all-night and Sunday pharmacies on their doors.

EMERGENCIES   For any emergency (fire, police, ambulance), the number is ☎ 112 from any land line or cellphone. For 24-hour urgent but nonemergency medical or dental service, call the **Central Doctors Service** (☎ 020/592-3434). **Residents of an E.U. country** must have a European Health Insurance Card to receive full reciprocal healthcare benefits in the Netherlands.

EVENT LISTINGS   **Time Out Amsterdam** is published monthly in English and lists all the happenings around

town. It's available at any newsstand for 2.95€.

FAMILY TRAVEL   The Amsterdam Tourist Information website has a family travel section that's very helpful: www.iamsterdam.com/en/ visiting/spotlight/family-kids.

GAY & LESBIAN TRAVELERS   **COC Amsterdam,** Rozenstraat 14 (☎ 020/ 626-3087; www.cocamsterdam.nl), is the local branch of the Dutch LGBT organization. It can answer any questions about anything gay in Holland. The city's largest gay and lesbian bookstore is **Boekhandel Vrolijk,** Paleisstraat 135 (☎ 020/623-5142; www.vrolijk.nu).

HOLIDAYS   National holidays include New Year's Day (Jan 1), Good Friday and Easter Monday (Mar or Apr), Queen's Day (Apr 30), Ascension Day (40 days after Easter), Pentecost Sunday (seventh Sun after Easter) and Pentecost Monday, Christmas Day (Dec 25), and Dec 26.

INSURANCE   North Americans with homeowner's or renter's insurance are probably covered for lost luggage. If not, inquire with **Travel Assistance International** (☎ 800/ 821-2828; www.travelassistance.com) or **Travelex** (☎ 800/228-9792; www. travelexinsurance.com), insurers that can also provide trip-cancellation, medical, and emergency evacuation coverage abroad. The website www.moneysupermarket. com compares prices across a wide range of providers for single- and multitrip policies. **For U.K. and Irish citizens,** insurance is always advisable, even if you have a European Health Insurance Card (see "Emergencies," above).

INTERNET ACCESS   Many hotels, coffeehouses (note that this generally doesn't mean pot-selling "coffee shops"), and other businesses offer Internet access. Dedicated cybercafes have virtually disappeared from the Amsterdam scene.

LIQUOR LAWS Supermarkets, grocery stores, and cafes sell alcoholic beverages. The legal drinking age is 16.

LOST PROPERTY If your luggage is lost, immediately file a lost-luggage claim at the airport, detailing the luggage contents. For most airlines, you must report delayed, damaged, or lost baggage within 4 hours of arrival.

MAIL & POST OFFICES Most offices of **TNT Post** (www.tntpost.nl) are open Monday to Friday from 9am to 5pm. The office at Singel 250, at the corner of Raadhuisstraat (tram 13, 14, or 17), is open Monday to Friday from 7:30am to 6pm, and Saturday from 7:30 to 9:30am. Stamps can usually be purchased from your hotel reception desk and at larger newsstands, especially ones that sell postcards.

MONEY The currency of the Netherlands is the euro, which can also be used in most other E.U. countries. The exchange rate varies, but at press time, 1 euro was equal to around US$1.41 and 0.88£. The best way to get cash in Amsterdam is at ATMs or cashpoints (see above). Credit cards are accepted at almost all hotels and many shops and restaurants, but you should always have some cash on hand for incidentals and sightseeing admissions.

NEWSPAPERS & MAGAZINES Most kiosks sell English-language newspapers, including the *International Herald Tribune, USA Today,* and British titles such as the *Times* and the *Guardian.*

PASSPORTS If your passport is lost or stolen, contact your country's embassy or consulate immediately (see "Consulates & Embassies," above). Before you travel, you should copy the critical pages and keep them separately from your passport.

POLICE Call ☎ 112 for emergencies. The most central police station is at Lijnbaansgracht 219 (☎ 0900/ 8844; tram 1, 2, 5, 7, or 10), just off Leidseplein.

SAFETY Be especially aware of child pickpockets. Their method is to get very close to a target, ask for a handout, and deftly help themselves to your money or passport. Robbery at gun- or knifepoint is very rare but not unknown. For more information, consult the U.S. State Department's website at www. travel.state.gov; in the U.K., consult the Foreign Office's website, www. fco.gov.uk; and in Australia, consult the government travel advisory service at www.smartraveller.gov.au.

SENIOR TRAVELERS Mention that you're a senior when you make your travel reservations. As in most cities, people 60 and older (in some places it may be 65 and older), qualify for reduced admission to Amsterdam theaters, museums, and other attractions, as well as discounted fares on public transportation.

SMOKING Smoking is common in Holland, but authorities are clamping down heavily on smoking in public places. It's long been banned in such places as theaters and on public transportation. Since 2008, smoking has been banned in hotel public spaces, restaurants, cafes, bars, and nightclubs (and other places), except in separate, enclosed smoking rooms where no food or drink is served by the staff.

TAXES Value-added tax, or VAT (BTW in the Netherlands) is 6% to 19%, depending on the amount and product you are purchasing, but non-E.U. visitors can get a refund if they spend 50€ or more in any store that participates in the VAT refund program. The shops will give you a form, which you must get stamped at Customs (allow extra time). Customs may ask to see your purchase, so don't pack it in your checked luggage. Mark the paperwork to request a credit card refund; otherwise, you'll be stuck with a check in euros.

TELEPHONES   Public phones, both coin-operated and those that take prepaid calling cards, are found in cafes, post offices, and on the street. Calling cards, available from kiosks and post offices, cost 5€, 10€, 20€, or 50€. For operator assistance, call ☎ 0800/0410. To make a **direct international call,** first dial 00, then dial the country code, the area code, and the local number. The country code for the **U.S. and Canada** is 1; **Great Britain,** 44; **Ireland,** 353; **Australia,** 61; and **New Zealand,** 64. To charge a call to your calling card, call **AT&T** (☎ 0800/022-9111), **Sprint** (☎ 0800/022-9119), **Canada Direct** (☎ 0800/022-9116), **British Telecom** (☎ 0800/022-9944), **Australia Direct** (☎ 0800/022-0061), or **Telecom New Zealand** (☎ 0800/022-4295).

TICKETS   The best outlet is the centrally located **Amsterdams Uitburo (AUB) Ticketshop,** Leidseplein 26 (☎ 0900/0191, or 31-20/621-1288 from outside the Netherlands; www.amsterdamsuitburo.nl). You can buy tickets on their website prior to your arrival. You can also ask your concierge to book tickets for you at the time you book your room.

TIPPING   In cafes and restaurants, waiter service is usually included, though you can round the bill up or leave some small change if you like. A service charge is included in taxi

fares, but a small tip (1€–2€) is always appreciated. If you make the driver wait or are going on a long, expensive trip, tip 5%. Tip hotel porters 1€ to 2€ for each piece of luggage.

TOILETS   If you use a toilet at a brown café or restaurant, it's customary to make some small purchase, or leave .50€.

TOURIST OFFICES   The best outlet is the office of Amsterdam Tourist Information at Stationsplein 10, right outside Centraal Station (☎ 020/201-8800; www.iamsterdam.com). A second office inside the station on platform 2 is closed long-term for rebuilding.

TOURS   The two largest tour companies are **Globus/Cosmos** (☎ 866/755-8581 or 800/276-1241; www.globusandcosmos.com) and **Trafalgar** (☎ 866/544-4434; www.trafalgar.com). Many major airlines offer air/land package deals that include tours of Amsterdam; ask the airlines or your travel agent for details.

TRAVELERS WITH DISABILITIES Nearly all modern hotels in Amsterdam now have rooms designed for people with disabilities, but many older hotels do not. Not all trams in Amsterdam are fully accessible for wheelchairs, but new trams have low central doors that are accessible. Amsterdam's Metro system is fully accessible.

Amsterdam: **A Brief History**

1200 Fishermen establish a settlement at the mouth of the Amstel River, which is subsequently dammed to control flooding; the settlement takes the name "Aemstelledamme."

1300 The bishop of Utrecht grants Amsterdam its first town charter.

1323 Amsterdam's economy receives a boost when it is declared a toll center for beer.

1350 The city becomes a transit point for imported grain, growing in importance as a trade center.

1602 The United East India Company (V.O.C.), destined to become a powerful force in Holland's Golden Age of discovery, exploration, and trade, is founded.

1611 First Amsterdam Stock Exchange opens.

1613 Construction begins on the Grachtengordel (Canal Ring), comprising the Herengracht, Keizersgracht, and Prinsengracht canals.

1631 Rembrandt, at age 25, moves to Amsterdam from his native Leiden.

1795 French troops occupy Holland with the aid of Dutch revolutionaries and establish the Batavian Republic; William V flees to England.

1806–10 Louis Bonaparte, Napoleon's brother, reigns as king of Holland.

1813 The Netherlands regains independence from the French.

1839 Holland's first rail line, connecting Amsterdam and Haarlem, opens.

1910 A flushable water system for the city's canals is introduced.

1920 Dutch airline KLM launches the world's first scheduled air service, between Amsterdam and London.

1928 The Olympics are held in Amsterdam.

1932 Afsluitdijk (Enclosure Dike) at the head of the Zuiderzee is completed, transforming the sea on which Amsterdam stands into the freshwater IJsselmeer lake.

1940 On May 10, Nazi Germany invades the Netherlands, which surrenders 4 days later.

1944–45 Thousands die during the Hunger Winter, when Nazi occupation forces blockade western Holland.

1945 On May 5, German forces in the Netherlands surrender.

1960s Amsterdam takes on the mantle of Europe's hippie capital.

1973 The Van Gogh Museum opens.

1975 Amsterdam's 700th anniversary. Cannabis use is decriminalized.

1987 The *Homomonument,* the world's first public memorial to persecuted gays and lesbians, is unveiled.

2001 The world's first same-sex marriage with a legal status identical to heterosexual matrimony takes place in Amsterdam.

2002 Euro bank notes and coins replace the guilder.

2004 Controversial film director Theo van Gogh is murdered by an Islamist extremist on the streets of Amsterdam.

2005 Homophobic assailants in Amsterdam beat up the editor of the *Washington Blade* LGBT newspaper.

2008 Smoking in restaurants, cafes, bars, and nightclubs is banned.

2010 The new Dutch coalition government announces plans to prevent foreign visitors from frequenting cannabis-selling "coffee shops."

Golden Age Art

Although there were earlier prominent Dutch artists, Dutch art really came into its own during the 17th-century Golden Age. Artists were blessed with wealthy patrons whose support allowed them to give free rein to their talents. The primary art patrons were Protestant merchants who commissioned portraits, genre scenes, and still lifes, not the kind of religious works commissioned by the church in Catholic countries. The Dutch were particularly fond of pictures that depicted their world: landscapes, seascapes, domestic scenes, and portraits.

Gerrit van Honthorst (1590–1656)

An Utrecht artist who had studied in Rome with Caravaggio, van Honthorst brought the new "realism of light and dark," or chiaroscuro, technique to Holland, where he influenced Dutch artists like the young Rembrandt. Van Honthorst is best known for lively company scenes such as *The Supper Party* (ca. 1620; Uffizi, Florence), which depicted ordinary people against a plain background and set a style that continued in Dutch art for many years. He often used multiple hidden light sources to heighten the dramatic contrast of lights and darks.

Jacob van Ruisdael (1628–82)

Among the great landscape artists of this period, van Ruisdael stands out. In his paintings, human figures either do not appear at all or are shown almost insignificantly small; vast skies filled with moody clouds often cover two-thirds of the canvas. His *Windmill at Wijk bij Duurstede* (ca.1665; Rijksmuseum, Amsterdam) combines many characteristic elements of his style. The windmill stands in a somber landscape, containing a few small human figures, with a cloud-laden sky and a foreground of agitated water and reeds.

Frans Hals (ca.1580–1666)

Antwerp-born Hals, the undisputed leader of the Haarlem school (schools differed from city to city), was a great portrait painter whose relaxed, informal, and naturalistic portraits contrast strikingly with the traditional formal masks of Renaissance portraits. His light brush strokes help convey immediacy and intimacy, making his works perceptive psychological portraits. He had a genius for comic characters, showing men and women as they are and a little less than they are, as in *Malle Babbe* (ca. 1635; Gemäldegalerie, Berlin). As a stage designer of group portraits, Hals's skill is almost unmatched—only Rembrandt is superior. Although he carefully arranged and posed each group, balancing the directions of gesture and glance, his *alla prima* brushwork (direct laying down of pigment) makes these public images seem spontaneous. It's worth taking a day trip to Haarlem just to visit the Frans Halsmuseum and view such works as his *A Banquet of the Officers of the St. George Civic Guard* (ca.1627) and *Officers and Sergeants of the St. Hadrian Civic Guard* (ca. 1633).

Rembrandt (1606–69)

The great genius of the period was Rembrandt Harmenszoon van Rijn, one of few artists of any period to be known simply by his first name. This painter, whose works hang in places of honor in the world's great galleries, may be *the* most famous

Amsterdammer, both to outsiders and to today's city residents.

Rembrandt pushed the art of chiaroscuro to unprecedented heights. In his paintings, the values of light and dark gradually and softly blend together; this may have diffused some of the drama of chiaroscuro, but it achieved a more truthful appearance. His art seems capable of revealing the soul and inner life of his subjects, and to view his series of 60 self-portraits is to see a remarkable documentation of his own psychological and physical evolution. The etching *Self-Portrait with Saskia* (1636; Rijksmuseum, Amsterdam) shows him with his wife at a prosperous time when he was being commissioned to do portraits of many wealthy merchants. Later self-portraits are more psychologically complex, often depicting a careworn old man whose gaze is nonetheless sharp, compassionate, and wise.

In group portraits like *The Night Watch* (1642) and *The Syndics of the Cloth Guild* (1662), both in the Rijksmuseum, each individual portrait is done with care. The unrivaled harmony of light, color, and movement of these works is a marvel to be appreciated. Compare, too, these robust, masculine works with the tender *The Jewish Bride* (ca. 1665), also in the Rijksmuseum.

In later years Rembrandt was at the height of his artistic powers, but his contemporaries judged his work to be too personal and eccentric. Some considered him a tasteless painter who was obsessed with the ugly and ignorant of color; this opinion prevailed until the 19th century, when Rembrandt's genius was reevaluated.

Jan Vermeer (1632–75)

Perhaps the best known of the "little Dutch masters" who specialized in one genre of painting, such as portraiture, is Jan Vermeer of Delft. Although they confined their artistry within a narrow scope, these painters rendered their subjects with an exquisite care and faithfulness to their actual appearances.

Vermeer's work centers on the simple pleasures and activities of domestic life—a woman pouring milk or reading a letter, for example—and all of his simple figures positively glow with color and light. Vermeer placed the figure (usually just one, but sometimes two or more) at the center of his paintings against a background in which furnishings often provided the horizontal and vertical balance, giving the composition a feeling of stability and serenity. Art historians have determined that Vermeer used mirrors and the camera obscura, an optical projection device, as compositional aids. A master at lighting interior scenes and rendering true colors, Vermeer was able to create an illusion of three-dimensionality in works such as *The Love Letter* (ca. 1670; Rijksmuseum, Amsterdam). As light—usually afternoon sunshine pouring in from an open window—moves across the picture plane, it caresses and modifies all the colors.

Jan Steen (ca. 1626–79)

Born in Leiden, Steen painted marvelous interior scenes, often satirical and didactic in their intent. The allusions on which much of the satire depends may escape most of us today, but any viewer can appreciate the fine drawing, subtle color shading, and warm light that pervades such paintings as *Woman at Her Toilet* (1663) and *The Feast of St. Nicholas* (ca. 1665), both in the Rijksmuseum, Amsterdam. Many of his pictures revel in bawdy tavern scenes fueled by overindulgence in beer and gin.

Useful Phrases & Menu Terms

Useful Words & Phrases

ENGLISH	DUTCH	PRONUNCIATION
Hello	Dag/Hallo	*dakh/ha-loh*
Good morning	Goedenmorgen	khoo-*yuh*-mor-khun
Good afternoon/ evening	Goedenavond	khoo-*yuhn*-af-*ond*
How are you?	Hoe gaat het met u?	*hoo* khaht et met oo?
Very well	Uitstekend	*out*-stayk-end
Thank you	Dank u wel	dahnk oo wel
Goodbye	Dag/Tot Ziens	*dakh/tot* zeenss
Good night	Goedenacht	khoo-*duh*-nakht
See you later	Tot straks	*Tot* strahkss
Please	Alstublieft	ahl-*stoo*-bleeft
Yes	Ja	*yah*
No	Neen/nee	*nay*
Excuse me	Pardon	*par*-dawn
Sorry	Sorry	so-*ree*
Do you speak English?	Spreekt u Engels?	*spraykt* oo eng-els
Can you help me?	Kunt u mij helpen?	*koont* oo may-ee hel-*pen*?
Give me . . .	Geeft U mij . . .	*khayft* oo may . . .
Where is . . . ?	Waar is . . . ?	vahr *iz* . . . ?
the station	het station	het stah-*ssyonh*
the post office	het postkantoor	het post-*kan-tohr*
a bank	een bank	*ayn* bank
a hotel	een hotel	*ayn* ho-*tel*
a restaurant	een restaurant	*ayn* res-to-*rahng*
a pharmacy/chemist	een apotheek	*ayn* a-po-*tayk*
the toilet	het toilet	het twah-*let*
To the right	Rechts	*rekhts*
To the left	Links	*links*
Straight ahead	Rechtdoor	*rekht*-doar
I would like . . .	Ik zou graag . . .	*ik zow khrakh* . . .
to eat	eten	ay-*ten*
a room for one night	een kamer voor een nacht willen	*ayn kah-mer voor ayn nakht wi-llen*
How much is it?	Hoe veel kost het?	*hoo fayl kawst het*
the check	de rekening	*duh* ray-ken-ing
When?	Wanneer?	*vah*-neer
yesterday	gisteren	khis-*ter*-en
today	vandaag	*van*-dahkh
tomorrow	morgen	mor-*khen*
breakfast	ontbijt	ohnt-*bayt*
lunch	lunch	*lunch*
dinner	diner	dee-*nay*

Numbers

ENGLISH	DUTCH	PRONUNCIATION
one	een	*ayn*
two	twee	*tway*
three	drie	*dree*
four	vier	*veer*
five	vijf	*vayf*
six	zes	*zes*
seven	zeven	*zay-vun*
eight	acht	*akht*
nine	negen	*nay-khen*
ten	tien	*teen*
eleven	elf	*elf*
twelve	twaalf	*tvahlf*
thirteen	dertien	dayr-*teen*
fourteen	veertien	vayr-*teen*
fifteen	vijftien	vayf-*teen*
sixteen	zestien	zes-*teen*
seventeen	zeventien	zay-*vun-teen*
eighteen	achttien	akh-*teen*
nineteen	negentien	nay-*khun-teen*
twenty	twintig	twin-*tikh*

Days of the Week

ENGLISH	DUTCH	PRONUNCIATION
Monday	Maandag	mahn-*dakh*
Tuesday	Dinsdag	deens-*dakh*
Wednesday	Woensdag	voohns-*dakh*
Thursday	Donderdag	donder-*dakh*
Friday	Vrijdag	vray-*dakh*
Saturday	Zaterdag	zahter-*dakh*
Sunday	Zondag	zohn-*dakh*

Months

ENGLISH	DUTCH	PRONUNCIATION
January	Januari	yahn-*oo-aree*
February	Februari	fayhb-*roo-aree*
March	Maart	*mahrt*
April	April	*ah*-pril
May	Mei	meh-*eey*
June	Juni	*yoo*-nee
July	Juli	*yoo*-lee
August	Augustus	*awh*-khoost-*oos*
September	September	*sep*-tem-*buhr*
October	Oktober	*oct*-oah-*buhr*
November	November	*noa*-vem-*buhr*
December	December	*day*-sem-*buhr*

Dutch Menu Savvy

BASICS

DUTCH	ENGLISH
ontbijt	breakfast
lunch	lunch
diner	dinner
voorgerechten	starters
hoofdgerechten	main courses
nagerechten	desserts
boter	butter
boterham	sandwich
brood	bread
stokbrood	French bread
honing	honey
hutspot	mashed potatoes and carrots, with onions
jam	jam
kaas	cheese
mosterd	mustard
pannenkoeken	pancakes
peper	pepper
zout	salt
suiker	sugar
saus	sauce

SOUPS (SOEPEN)

DUTCH	ENGLISH
soep	soup
aardappelsoep	potato soup
bonensoep	bean soup
erwtensoep	pea soup (usually includes bacon or sausage)
groentesoep	vegetable soup
kippensoep	chicken soup
uiensoep	onion soup
tomatensoep	tomato soup

EGGS (EIEREN)

DUTCH	ENGLISH
eier	egg
hardgekookte eieren	hard-boiled eggs
zachtgekookte eieren	soft-boiled eggs
omelette	omelet
roereieren	scrambled eggs
spiegeleieren	fried eggs
uitsmijter	fried eggs and ham on bread

FISH (VIS)

DUTCH	ENGLISH
forel	trout
garnalen	prawns
gerookte zalm	smoked salmon
haring	herring
kabeljauw	cod
kreeft	lobster
makreel	mackerel
mosselen	mussels
oesters	oysters
paling	eel
sardientjes	sardines
schelvis	haddock
schol	plaice
tong	sole
zalm	salmon

MEATS (VLEES)

DUTCH	ENGLISH
rundvlees	beef
biefstuk	steak
eend	duck
fricandeau	roast pork
gans	goose
gehakt	minced meat
haasbiefstuk	filet steak
ham	ham
kalfsvlees	veal
kalkoen	turkey
kip	chicken
konijn	rabbit
lamsvlees	lamb
lamskotelet	lamb chops
ragout	beef stew
rookvlees	smoked meat
lever	liver
spek	bacon
vleeswaren	cold cuts
worst	sausage

VEGETABLES & SALADS (GROENTEN/SLA)

DUTCH	ENGLISH
groenten	vegetables
asperges	asparagus
augurken	pickles
bieten	beets
bloemkool	cauliflower
bonen	beans
champignons	mushrooms
erwten	peas
aardappelen	potatoes
knoflook	garlic
komkommer	cucumber
komkommersla	cucumber salad
kool	cabbage
patates frites	french fries
prei	leek
prinsesseboonen	green beans
purée	mashed potatoes
radijsjes	radishes
rapen	turnips
rijst	rice
sla	lettuce, salad
spinazie	spinach
tomaten	tomatoes
uien	onions
wortelen	carrots
zuurkool	sauerkraut

DESSERTS (NAGERECHTEN)

DUTCH	ENGLISH
appelgebak	apple pie
appelmoes	applesauce
cake	cake
compote	stewed fruits
gebak	pastry/cake
ijs	ice cream
oliebollen	doughnuts
koekjes	cookies
jonge kaas	young cheese (mild)
oude kaas	mature cheese (strong)
room	cream
slagroom	whipped cream
smeerkaas	cheese spread
speculaas	spiced cookies

FRUITS (VRUCHTEN)

DUTCH	ENGLISH
aardbei	strawberry
ananas	pineapple
appel	apple
citroen	lemon
druiven	grapes
framboos	raspberry
kersen	cherries
peer	pear
perzik	peach
pruimen	plums

BEVERAGES (DRANKEN)

DUTCH	ENGLISH
bier (or pils)	beer
cognac	brandy
fles	bottle
glas	glass
jenever	gin
koffie	coffee
melk	milk
rode wijn	red wine
thee	tea
water	water
mineraal water	sparkling water
witte wijn	white wine

COOKING TERMS

DUTCH	ENGLISH
gebakken	baked/fried
gebraden	roast
gegrild	grilled
gekookt	boiled/cooked
gerookt	smoked
geroosterd	roasted/toasted
gestoofd	stewed/braised
goed doorbakken	well done
half doorbakken	medium
koud	cold
niet doorbakken	rare
warm	hot

Index

See also Accommodations and Restaurant indexes, below.

Photo **Credits**

Notes

Notes